ABOUT THE AUTHORS

Joan Reid Ahrens is an American graduate gemologist living in Hong Kong. She was raised as an Air Force dependent and continues to travel the globe with her businessman husband and four children. She has been involved with the study of gemstones for more than twelve years and has visited mining and buying centres in Brazil, Asia and the US. She currently serves as a board member for both the Hong Kong Gemologists Association and the Gemmological Association of Hong Kong as well as contributing articles to local trade publications.

Ruth Lor Malloy is a freelance writer, a novelist and the author of travel guides to Hong Kong and China. A Canadian of Chinese ancestry, she has been exploring the markets of Asia since 1960 as a resident of Japan, Thailand, the Philippines, Vietnam, India, and now Hong Kong.

Gems & Jewellery in Hong Kong
A Buyer's Guide

by
Joan Reid Ahrens, GG, and Ruth Lor Malloy

Published by the South China Morning Post
Publications Division, Tong Chong Street,
Quarry Bay, Hong Kong.

Set in Bodoni Book type by Filmset Ltd.

Printed by Yee Ting Tong Printing Press Ltd.

ISBN 962 10 0029 7

ACKNOWLEDGEMENTS

The authors are grateful for the generous help of many friends, jewellers and gemmologists who gave suggestions and information for this book, and to Gillian Kellogg for her help in editing.

Our thanks also go to our families who made sacrifices so we could complete this work.

Cover photo by Roy C.
Jewellery from Joan Ahrens and
Hannah Zion

CONTENTS

Introduction 9

Buying

  Buying in Hong Kong 17

  Preparing Yourself for Buying 18

  The Reliable Jeweller 18

  Buying Techniques 21

  Synthetics and Imitations 39

  The Doctoring of Gems 41

Gems 42

  Agate and Jasper 47

  Amethyst 48

  Aquamarine 50

  Cat's Eye Chrysoberyl 52

  Citrine 53

  Coral 55

  Diamond 56

  Emerald 64

  Garnet 67

  Goldstone 70

  Ivory 70

  Jade 75

  Lapis lazuli 80

  Malachite 81

  Opal 83

  Pearl 85

  Peridot 92

  Quartz 93

  Ruby 96

  Sapphire 98

Sodalite 101
Topaz 102
Tourmaline 105
Turquoise 107

More on Buying
Before You Buy Jewellery 109
Made to Order Jewellery 113
Local Jewellery Designers 114
Foreign Imports 115
Antique Jewellery 116
Carvings 118
Settings and Metals 118
Shopping for Other People 127
Gemmologists as Guides 127
Jewellery for Men 128
Care and Protection of Jewellery 129
Repairing, Polishing and Cleaning 131
Replacing a Gem 132

Economics
Insurance and Appraisals 134
Gems and Jewellery as Investments 137

Appendix
Customs Regulations 139
Consulates and Commissions 142
Addresses 143
Colour Chart 151
Birthstones 153
Mohs Hardness Scale 154
Chinese Calligraphy in Jewellery 155
Glossary 156
Bibliography 159

INTRODUCTION

You're in Hong Kong. You've heard that jewellery and gems here are great bargains. You've never seen so many jewellery stores. They are filled with colour, shapes and texture like miniature fruits in a supermarket and with what look to you like a fortune in Imperial jade. You've heard that this is the best place in the world to buy jade and jewellery.

You are tempted but hesitate. The stones are huge, beautiful and dazzling. Labour is cheaper here than in Western countries, you reason, but what about quality? How do you know this diamond is really a diamond? Just because this friendly store clerk says so? Could this "emerald" be green glass made from a Coke bottle? Could this "sapphire" be one of the synthetics you've read about that even experts have difficulty identifying?

If this ruby is natural, it would make Susie's eyes light up. It's half the price of the one you saw in the hotel and everyone knows how high rents are there. *Are* they all that high? What about the commissions to tourist guides?

But, *if* you buy and you *later* discover it's not natural, you could be miserable. If you don't buy, will it ruin the rest of your trip wondering if you should have? And what about this "haggling" you've been told about? How is this done?

★★★

Based on our observations and experiences exploring other parts of the world, **we find Hong Kong ideal for jewellery shopping** because:

● There is a **better selection** here than elsewhere in Asia for some gems such as diamonds, rubies, sapphires, emeralds and jade. Many stores carry amethysts, aquamarines, blue topaz, cat's eyes, citrines, garnets, opals, peridots, smoky quartz and tourmalines (especially pinks). You may also find a ready supply of decorative stones such as malachite, lapis lazuli, sodalite, agate, chrysoprase, onyx etc. as well as a vast quantity of ivory, pearls and coral.

● Hong Kong is the third or fourth **major jewellery and gem centre in the world,** and it is also the third largest diamond trading centre. It exports diamonds to Japan, and fine and costume jewellery to the US. It exports more watches than Switzerland and at the same time is that country's second largest customer for gold and custom-made watches.

● The prices are good here because there are **no sales taxes or import duties** on gems and jewellery.

● **You can dicker over prices.** The person who understands this business can acquire a super bargain. Others achieve fine values.

● There are **long established markets** here—local, visitor and export. Hong Kong has developed a high level of sophistication in workmanship and design.

● It offers the discriminating buyer a wide range of **imported European designed jewellery** seldom seen in the same city anywhere in the world.

About 400 manufacturers and wholesalers of gems and jewellery are listed in the yellow pages of the Business Telephone Directory. Count them. These supply more than 1,000 local retail jewellery stores.

Competition is fierce. Many merchants rely on volume selling to make their profit. Others sell consignment goods at small profits. If you have the time and inclination, you can purchase top merchandise at close to wholesale export prices.

But what are the risks? Buying gems and jewellery anywhere can be risky if you don't know what you're doing or from whom you are buying. You could be overcharged, sold a fake or given third-rate goods.

So you admit you don't know what you're doing? Don't worry. You are in the majority and you can learn. Your cries for help have not gone unheard. Here are some guidelines that have worked for us and many others while shopping in Hong Kong.

But **why not wait** until you get to Bangkok to buy sapphires and rubies, and Rangoon to buy jade?

● Because synthetics and imitations, complete with guarantees and certificates of natural origin, abound in Bangkok. You must know your stores there too. Hong Kong's track record is much better, and guarantees are backed by trade and government agencies.

● Because very little finished jade, of good quality, is for sale in Burma to the casual visitor. Most of it is exported in the rough to places like Hong Kong. Here it is finished, put on the local market or exported to other countries, including Thailand and Singapore.

● Because **the overall quality of gems and jewellery available here is better.** Stone cutting costs may be less in other countries like India, Sri Lanka and Thailand, but the cutting is generally poor. Professional buyers from Hong Kong go to these countries and buy the top quality stones before they reach the local market. Many of these stones have to be re-cut and polished here to meet international standards set by the buying public.

● Because Hong Kong is the only place in Asia, with the exception of costly Japan, that has any **effective consumer protection.** Please read the section on the Hong Kong Tourist Association and the Diamond Importers' Association under *The Reliable Jeweller, page 18.*

Guidelines for Buying in Hong Kong

Now that you know why to buy in Hong Kong, try to answer "yes" to all the following questions while deciding on a purchase. If you can, your chances for a successful shopping expedition are assured. See the sections in parentheses for more information. Read these now in anticipation of later decisions when you are actually confronted with having to buy gems or jewellery.

1. Do you have *some* idea of the prices for comparable jewellery, diamonds or coloured stones in your home country? *(Preparing Yourself for Buying, page 18)*
2. Did you make a shopping list with a price range in Hong Kong dollars so you would know how much you could spend on any particular item before you entered a store? *(Buying Techniques, page 21)* Don't let foreign currency exchange calculations confuse you. Calculators are cheap here. Buy one if necessary.
3. Have you gone over every point in our relevant gem section and checked it against the gem you hope to buy? *(Gems, page 42)*
4. Are the gems you have selected in our list of popularly traded gems? *(Gems)*
5. If you are considering jewellery, have you absorbed our section *Before You Buy Jewellery, page 109*?
6. Have you satisfied the requirements listed on finding a reliable jeweller? *(The Reliable Jeweller, page 18)*
7. Have you avoided tour bus stores? *(The Reliable Jeweller)* Or did you even notice one?
8. Do local residents also buy in this store? *(The Reliable Jeweller)*
9. Did you give the impression that you have local connections? *(Buying Techniques)*
10. Did you use an introduction, even if it was this book? *(Buying Techniques)*
11. Is this store a member of the Hong Kong Tourist Association or Diamond Importers' Association? *(The Reliable Jeweller)*
12. If your purchase is over HK$25,000, did you deal with the manager? *(Buying Techniques)*

13. Did you inspect each major gem with a loupe, or magnifying glass? *(Buying Techniques)*
14. Did you look for chips, scratches, poor proportions etc.? *(Buying Techniques)*
15. If the gem is set in gold, did you find the manufacturer's logo and gold fineness stamp on it? *(Settings, page 124)*
16. In the case of faceted gems, did you check to see that the cutting lines were straight, proportions pleasing to the eye, that facet junctions met, no "fish eyes" or "windows" etc.? *(Buying Techniques)*
17. Did you examine the gem in the proper light? *(Buying Techniques)*
18. Did you compare the selected gem with more expensive higher quality gems? *(Buying Techniques)*
19. Did you compare prices and qualities in other stores? *(Buying Techniques)*
20. Did you haggle for a lower price? And did you get 20 to 60 percent off? *(Buying Techniques)*
21. Were prices clearly marked in Hong Kong dollars? *(The Reliable Jeweller)*
22. Was pertinent data listed on tags attached to the gem or jewellery? Carat weight of diamonds and gems, number of grams of gold and gold fineness? *(The Reliable Jeweller)*
23. If a shopkeeper was rude, did you let his bullying affect your decision? *(Buying Techniques)*
24. Did you use some jewellers' vocabulary and impress the shopkeeper? *(Buying Techniques)*
25. Can you obtain a satisfactory guarantee with return-exchange policy in writing and a detailed receipt? *(Buying Techniques)*
26. If your purchase is over HK$5,000, did you seriously consider having the gems tested by an impartial gemmologist? *(Buying Techniques)*
27. Are you aware of the Customs regulations in your own country as well as those you will be passing through on this

trip? Are you aware that some gem materials could be confiscated? *(Appendix, page 139)*

NOTE

We have visited all the stores mentioned in this book. Many have been recommended by long-time expatriate residents and local Chinese. Most are members of the HKTA or the DIA. At press time we do not hesitate to recommend them. However, because of possible changes in management and staff, there may be changes in the quality of service. We ask that you make *your own* assessment and offer this book as a *guide only* to help in your shopping expeditions. We acknowledge the probability of many more reliable stores that we have not had the opportunity to research. We welcome learning of your adventures, both good and bad, while buying jewellery in Hong Kong. Please tell us about *your* favourite stores. Perhaps we will include them in future editions.

We wish you happy, fruitful and pleasant jewellery shopping in what we consider to be the best location in the world.

Joan Reid Ahrens, and Ruth Lor Malloy

PS: We must apologise that space does not permit us to use both genders. Shopkeepers, jewellery lovers and Customs officials come in male and female varieties.

Note also: All prices mentioned are in Hong Kong dollars unless otherwise noted. These are intended only as guidelines. DO NOT point to them and tell your jeweller, "It says here that a pearl of that sort shouldn't cost that much!"

Prices are not that simple. There are just too many factors involved, including size, quality, availability and foreign exchange rates. We can only tell you what we think is fair in mid-1983. Even two months later, the picture could be completely different. Hong Kong's exchange rate has ranged in the last year from $5.7 to $9.5 to the US dollar, and is now officially stabilised at $7.80. Our dollar quotes were calculated roughly at $6.9 but even then they are only rough estimates based on personal observations and quotes from business associates.

BUYING

Buying in Hong Kong

In addition to its "bargain" prices, enormous selection, high quality and consumer protection, Hong Kong has some other notable peculiarities.

1. "Duty free" here is misleading. Everything in Hong Kong is duty free except for perfume, liquor, cigarettes, cars and petroleum products.

2. Tourists spend almost as much on jewellery as on clothing, the two most popular shopping categories.

3. Some store clerks can seem rude to our way of thinking. From time to time the HKTA runs courtesy campaigns, giving awards for what should come naturally. Some clerks appear rude because they cannot handle English well. Some are watching for possible shoplifting and create an air of tension. Others are rude because of the tremendous pressure on them — the high rents, competition, construction noises, crowded living conditions or uncertain future. They may also be inadequately trained or just tired.

4. Another local peculiarity, contrary to the above, is that some clerks have, in common with clerks all over East Asia, the tendency to say "yes, yes" in situations where one might expect a "no". One reason is that they do not fully understand your questions, yet want to be pleasant and positive. So they nod and say "yes". Most stores you will be frequenting will have clerks with a good command of English, so this will not be a serious problem. But it might occur.

Another reason for the apparent affirmatives is the clerks' desire to make you happy with their store. They may try to satisfy you even to the point of talking you into buying something you didn't want to buy in the first place — the super sell.

Read our section on *Buying* very carefully.

Preparing Yourself for Buying

This should start before you go to a store — or even before you come to Hong Kong.

If you are serious about making a good buy while here, first consult a jeweller at home. Price everything you think you might buy abroad. Note down weight, sizes, colours (using words that you can relate to like fire-engine red, strawberry pink, pea green, lemon yellow and periwinkle blue) and GIA rating of diamonds.

Study stones wherever you can. Price the settings in 14K and 18K gold, and break down the cost into gold, labour and individual stones. Ask about synthetics.

Your jeweller may be reluctant to co-operate. After all, he may be losing a sale. He will probably warn you to be careful. He may relate an incident like, "Mrs Phillips returned from Istanbul last year with a five-carat sapphire which turned out to be synthetic and cost her $4,000!" The warning is not unfounded. But Mrs Phillips obviously wasn't careful. Nor did she follow the tips in this book.

Acquaint yourself with the best of gems beforehand at gem shows, museums and fine jewellery stores. A handy paperback, *Gems and Jewelry* by Joel Arem, is an excellent supplementary guide with vivid colour plates.

When you get to Hong Kong, look for a reliable dealer if you want value for money. This is your primary protection, so do take time to find him.

The Reliable Jeweller

is preferably one who:

● has been in business in Hong Kong **at least a decade** or so.

● is **not on the tourist bus route.** Tour bus-patronised shops tend to be overpriced, at least for the local or expatriate resident. These shops can usually be spotted because they sell all kinds of other souvenirs and are heavily staffed with solicitous clerks. Some also have prices marked in US dollars and a prominent foreign exchange conversion chart displayed.

However, the presence of a lot of tourists in a store does not mean that the store is to be avoided. It might mean that several tourists have discovered a store they like and have told their friends. After all, Hong Kong teems with tourists.

● **caters to local residents.** You could survey your hotel concierge, consulate, travel agent, beauty salon operator, restaurant manager, cruise ship recreation director, dinner partner, business associates and locally-based friends. One problem is that one or two of these people might get commissions from the shops they recommend, therefore compare prices whenever possible.

If you're friendly with a bank manager, ask him if he can recommend a store so that you can be sure that the six months guarantee you hope to get will be from a store that will still be in business then.

● **is careful with his gems.** He doesn't abuse them by putting them all in one dish or tray to become scratched or chipped. An excellent system for viewing individual gems is a tray of forty or more 2″ padded, plastic boxes from which clients can select one at a time to view at close range. Pertinent data about the gem should be on the flip side on a gummed label. Many jewellers will have their gems in diamond papers of no more than a half-dozen stones each. Sometimes the paper is lined with cotton for added protection.

● **will have the proper kind of lighting** for examining gems and allow you to take a stone outside to view in daylight if there is no window. Blue light, for example, makes diamonds look deceptively good.

● will have a **jeweller's loupe,** a 10X magnifying glass and tweezers available for you to use.

● will allow you to take a gem to an **independent gem-mologist** for verification and refund your money if he has given you a misrepresented stone. This guarantee must be in writing.

● will not pressure you to buy anything.

You should consider choosing your jeweller with the same care you would take in selecting a nursery school. Just as you would question the school's reputation and qualifications for your child's first school experience by asking trusted friends or calling the Better Business Bureau, so you must find out about your jeweller.

It is easier to find a reliable jeweller by narrowing the field to membership in the **Hong Kong Tourist Association** or the **Diamond Importers' Association.** There are many reliable dealers who are not members of either, but unless you have time for much research, use these memberships as your yardstick.

The Hong Kong Tourist Association

Retail stores can join this government-sponsored body as associate members by meeting membership requirements. All retail members are listed in *The Official Guide to Shopping, Eating Out and Services in Hong Kong.* Ask for it in any HKTA office if it is not available at your hotel. (See *Appendix, page 150.*) While it may be possible to have some unreliable HKTA members, you do have clout if you have a grievance.

Only HKTA stores are allowed to display the association's sailing junk symbol, shown opposite. When membership is questioned, some clerks will pretend that their store is a member. "We just joined. We haven't received our sticker yet."

When you are deciding on an expensive purchase, it might be wise to excuse yourself and take time for some thought. **Make a telephone call to the membership department of the HKTA** and ask if the shop is indeed a member and if there have been any complaints registered against it. If the store is not a member, try the **Consumer Council,** which is a government-funded, private consumer protection agency. If you're satisfied with the answers to your queries, return to the store and give bargaining another try.

The Hong Kong Tourist Association aims for "reliable information and polite service, good value for money, accurate representation of products sold, and prompt rectification of justified complaints". It does police its member stores. It "requires all its gold-trading members to mark every gold or gold-alloyed item displayed or offered for sale with marks indicating the gold fineness of the article and the identity of the shop/manufacturer".

The HKTA is interested in learning about any discourteous service or unfair pricing in any of its member stores.

Please note that written guarantees are only worth the paper they are printed on coupled with the reputation of the shop, unless backed by organisations such as the HKTA.

Buying Techniques

1. Determine what you want to buy. Take a cursory first look at a few shops and make notes of prices and quality. Later, back in your room, do some thinking. Would another ruby ring be practical? Would it be better to buy ruby earrings and make a set? Would sapphires match her eyes? Her favourite dress? What's his birthstone?

For the same price, you could get better quality in rubies or most other gems if you bought several smaller stones rather than one big one. Do you want to do that?

High quality goods are always the better choice, and will last a lifetime. The inexpensive "bargains" will weather the trip home and then may begin to shed prongs, change colour or become unglued as fast as you lose your fading tan.

2. Seriously consider hiring a shopping guide if you are short of time, hate to shop or have expensive tastes. Graduate or near-graduate gemmologists, knowledgeable about the local market, can be contacted through the author, Joan Ahrens. They may be hired to work on a daily or hourly basis and will probably save you time, money and anxiety. See *Gemmologists as Guides, page 127.*

3. Store opening hours range from 9:30 to 11:00 am and closing from 6:00 to 10:30 pm. Hours differ according to location. Telephone first if you have a specific store in mind. Many stores are open Sundays, especially on the Kowloon side. Shops are packed then, however, with local residents and tourists alike. Check the store's location from a free HKTA map available in hotels or from an HKTA office.

4. If you have a specific requirement, use the telephone. If the person on the other end has difficulty communicating in English, ask the room boy or resident manager in your hotel to help.

5. If you want unset stones, wholesalers often have the best selection. Call first. If you do contact a wholesaler, just remember that he *usually* sells in large quantities or lot sales. His transactions can involve tens of thousands of dollars. If he agrees to sell you a couple of selected stones, cash is a must. No credit cards. Don't be offended by his directness. On the phone be as specific in your request as possible: e.g. "I am looking for an oval tanzanite between three and five carats of a medium violet blue colour with few inclusions. I want a stone that has sparkle, is well cut, and between $15,000 to $18,000."

A dealer should know immediately if he has such a stone or where he can acquire one for your inspection, thus saving you the trouble.

A dealer realises that when you are vague in your request, you do not know much about gems or what you want. He will therefore not be anxious to show you his inventory only to have you become confused and walk out empty-handed. Wholesalers in general are not the patient gentlemen found in retail stores, selling one stone at a time at appropriate mark-ups. See addresses in *Appendix, page 148*.

Many retail shops do carry unset gems and will with some reluctance show them to you. Many jewellers are not opposed to removing a stone from a setting and selling it separately.

6. Dress the part. Jeans or shorts, tee-shirt, camera and map give the impression that you have included gem stores as part of your sightseeing. The clerk will show you a few pieces and quote prices, but if you don't appear very interested he may go off to tend to another customer.

If you are serious about locating a rare five-carat Burmese ruby, for example, you might put on a nicer outfit than the one used for going to the outdoor jade market. Local merchants are very good at meeting your requests but they have to decide if you are serious or not.

7. Take a copy of this book with you when you go to buy. It can serve as your guide and as an introduction to the stores suggested. Eventually, it will become compulsory reading for them as well. Sample approach: "We found your address in this book. It says that you sell fine pearls and I can expect good value for my money." Because all the businesses listed are done so free of charge and because of the potential for increased sales, we feel prices should become lower and "games" be diminished. But do haggle. There is always some leeway.

8. Introductions are very important to the Chinese. They tend to honour referrals and those who sent them more than strangers coming in cold.

If you have no introduction and see a store you want to try, you might want to play our game: "Bill Drumright from Sydney told me he shops here every trip and you always give him a good price. He showed us the six emeralds and three rubies he bought from you on his last trip." Please change the name and particulars to fit your own situation, as these are exaggerated, but this will give you the technique.

This ploy will almost always work, as the shopkeeper does not want to give you a bad deal on a recommendation for fear an old customer will learn about it and not return, even though he may not place the name. Who remembers names of last year's customers?

If you are interested in diamonds, you can get an Introduction Card from the Diamond Importers' Association, whose members should give you a discount but are not obligated to do so. Bargaining is still in order. This card must be obtained in person from the association's office. Presentation of your passport is proof that you're a tourist. See page 150 for the address.

9. Above all, to get the best prices, **do not give the impression that you are a tourist without local connections.** Tourists become the target of every shopkeeper from the sleazy to the most affluent with their ready cash, reluctance to haggle and lack of familiarity with products, prices and quality levels. These, combined with lack of time to grasp the local market and to do a fair job of comparison shopping, give the retailer the advantage.

Your chances of getting a good buy increase if: (a) you are introduced by a friend who buys regularly at this store; (b) the friend introduces you in person or by telephone to a particular clerk or the manager; (c) you live in Hong Kong; (d) you work for a large multinational corporation which has many employees and visitors all anxious to know where to buy jewellery; (e) you speak Cantonese and (f) have a sense of humour.

In other words, you are *important*, have *potential*, and are a *personal friend* of a good customer whom they want to keep happy. You can't lose, or can you? **Don't ever ignore common sense and our guidelines.** All this depends on how knowledgeable about jewellery your mutual friend is, and how honourable the shop.

You must also realise that **discounting is a way of life** in most Asian countries. Europeans, Americans and Australians may find it distasteful but it is expected here and *can* be a lot of fun!

"We don't want to do it," said one distinguished jeweller, "but our customers get angry if we don't. So we mark up our prices to include a discounting factor."

10. Speak jewellers' language as much as possible. This will give the impression you know something about jewellery and should not be dismissed lightly. If the shopkeeper is thinking of showing you anything questionable, he will probably refrain from doing so.

But be careful. This ploy might get out of hand. He might test *you*. Don't ask about green garnets and then wonder why the clerk says he doesn't have any "demantoids" or "tsavolites". You should have known that demantoids and tsavolites *are* green garnets.

Look around the store. If you like his diamonds, then say something like, "I'm looking for a three-quarter carat, G, VVS1 diamond. What can you show me?" You can learn "jeweller's talk" simply by absorbing this book and listening to jewellers.

11. Establish that you are not in any rush to buy. e.g. "My friend wanted me to look at . . ." or "I just want to get some idea of prices . . ." This gives you an easy out if you don't want to buy in that store.

12. Take your time. Most stores have stools for your

comfort. Some even provide tea or soft drinks for your revival during the warm months. We have never felt obligated for these considerations although they have been welcome. Don't give the impression you have to have *that* particular piece and no other. Don't appear rushed. Act indifferent. Act Chinese. Control your excitement.

13. Don't feel that you have to buy at the first store. "I have to consult my husband" usually results in a cheerful, understanding "okay". Do take the shop's business card and even note the name of the clerk and the prices if you have any intention of returning. If something is being held for you and you buy elsewhere, do have the courtesy to telephone your decision. Better still, when you have a store "hold" a piece for you, put a time limit on it.

14. Find out early in the game the shop's return and guarantee policy. You may want to have your prospective purchase tested by an independent gemmologist. Or you may want to show it to a busy spouse. You should be able to take it on approval. Pay the store and get a detailed receipt stating that your money will be refunded if the gem is returned within a limited time in the same condition as when it left the store. *But you must get it in writing.* Aside from that, most jewellers will take back gems and jewellery they have sold you, *but only for credit.* Most sales receipts say "goods not refundable". Make sure you know what this means.

What if Wanda doesn't like it? Wanda is in Frankfurt. Can you get a refund or exchange it by mail or bring it on your next trip? What if you want to trade it back for a better stone later? It is obvious that the store's policy will influence your decision to buy there or not.

Some stores have successfully made **exchanges by mail**. However, no postal system is 100 percent reliable and it is advisable to send valuable parcels by registered airmail, insured (maximum $2,000), "return receipt requested" where applicable. If the gems are over that limit, insure through a

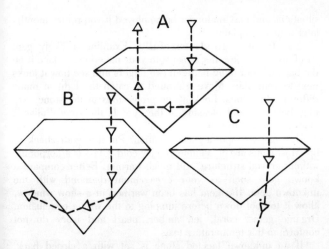

Reflection of light in diamonds. (A) A properly cut gem will refract light back through the crown producing brilliance. (B) A gem cut too deeply will lose light out of the side. (C) A gem cut too shallow will lose light through the bottom. Facet angles, refractive indices, polish and proportions all contribute to brilliancy in other gems.

private insurance company.

Returned goods must be in the same condition as sold. However, who is to decide if the goods received are "damaged"? And who "done" it? The mailman? You may be thousands of miles away, unable to assess the extent of the "damage" claimed by the shop. To avoid this it is better that you take the time to make a good choice now.

The store must be willing to put into writing whatever you agree on verbally unless you have dealt with a trusted manager for years. A manager's signature is double protection. A salesperson may not have authority in special situations and may no longer be employed if you return months later with a complaint.

15. Inspect goods carefully. Examine a likely gem carefully over a jeweller's pad with your naked eye. Place it on the back of your hand between two fingers and see how it looks next to your skin. Move it around to catch the light in many different directions. Look at the *proportions* of the stone. Are they balanced and pleasing to the eye? Is the stone "alive"? Does it "speak" to you?

How can you spot a glass imitation? Put it to your cheek or lip. Most gems are crystalline and icy cold. Glass is amorphous, without crystal structure, and much warmer. Better compare a known gem such as your engagement diamond with the unknown gem. If a gem has been warmed in a show window, allow it to cool down before jumping to the wrong conclusion. Organic gems, coral, jet, amber, pearl and ivory do not conform to this temperature test.

If an unknown faceted stone is set with a closed back, something may be amiss. A natural stone does not need a metallic backing to reflect light back or deepen colour. Glass does. A gold bezel surrounding the girdle of the stone may hide the seams of a doublet or triplet.

You would never find an expensive gem in a cheap-looking base-metal setting. Look for stones glued in metal depressions which are common for "paste" or glass imitations.

Next ask to view the gem with a loupe, a 10X magnifying lens, standard equipment for all gemmologists and jewellers. For a loose stone, ask for a pair of tweezers to hold the gem. With the lens in one hand close to your eye, bring the tweezers towards it until the gem is in focus.

A jeweller will know immediately if you are using a loupe correctly and can only guess how much you know about gems. If you buy a lot of jewellery, you may want to invest in a loupe of your own. They can be purchased locally for $100 to $200. See *Appendix, page 149.*

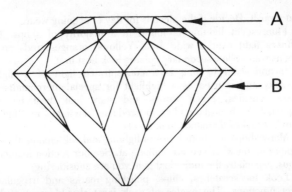

Doublets are not always meant to deceive, but buyers should be aware of them and pay accordingly. In this case a garnet top (A) has been fused onto a glass bottom (B).

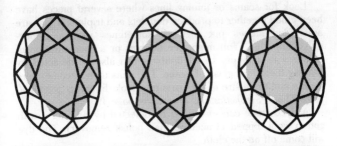

Garnet doublet from the top showing how a piece of genuine garnet (shaded portion) can be fused into a glass base.

Needless to say, **proper lighting** is important. Daylight is preferred but since artificial light improves the colour of many stones, inspect your stone in fluorescent, incandescent and natural lighting as you will probably encounter all three when you wear it. Decide if the piece is for day or evening wear.

Fluorescent lighting is found in a majority of shops. It diffuses light over a wide area. Yellows, oranges, reds and greens with yellow secondary colours look best in it.

Incandescent lighting is a concentrated light of a high intensity and is used as a highlight for special merchandise. Blues, purples, green stones and stars look best in it. Especially with a glass filter to produce "daylight" or "light blue", it makes diamonds look great.

Many shops use both types of lighting and will change them depending on what you are looking at. See our section headed *Gems*, especially the individual gem you are considering.

Look for scratches, chips, polishing marks and irregular facet junctions. The angles of each facet should meet each other neatly on a well-cut gem. Look for inclusions and fractures that come to the surface and could cause the stone to break during setting, especially in emeralds and opals.

Look for seams or joining lines where several pieces have been glued together to produce doublets and triplets. These are assembled stones put together sometimes with a colour-enhancing glue. You might see bubbles or a concentration of colour with a loupe. Unset doublets can also be detected by placing them in a glass of water. The joins then become more visible and the lustre of the parts may look different. See *Opal, page 83* and *Synthetics and Imitations, page 39*.

A dyed stone can *sometimes* be detected by rubbing it with cotton wool dipped in acetone (nail polish remover). The dye will come off on the cloth.

You will probably not be able to interpret inclusions unless you have studied gemmology. But there is no reason for you to accept a damaged or poorly cut stone. A scratched or nicked stone can be repolished in a matter of hours. It should cost nothing extra. In your home country it would probably cost a tidy sum to have it done, so insist that it be done here.

In gold jewellery, look for the shop hallmark and gold

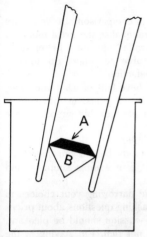

Water test for frequently found doublets. Notice the difference in colour of the two parts when viewed from the side: (A) garnet, (B) coloured glass.

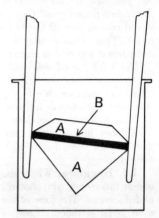

Water test for emerald triplet. (A) Colourless quartz or spinel; (B) green adhesive.

fineness stamp. See *Settings, page 124.*

Do not examine more than three tine stones at a time. To view more becomes confusing. As additional ones are offered, put one aside, keeping only three in front of you until you have seen them all. Compare the polish, brilliance, flaws, colours, all of the characteristics we have already mentioned. Then choose the best from these last three.

16. Before you decide on a purchase, review the section on the gem you are considering, especially for best lighting, simple tests and counterfeits. Go over the check list in the *Introduction.*

Compare your chosen gem with a more expensive stone.

Are you thrilled with your choice in comparison? Do you covet the higher-priced gem? Can you rationalise the extra money it would cost to own it? Could you trade "up" for a better stone later? Your choice should be able to stand up to this comparison test *now* to ensure satisfaction.

Don't fall for all sales talk. Believe half of what you hear. When questioning the origin of certain gems, we often hear, "You can trust us. We buy from old, reliable suppliers. We don't sell synthetics or imitations."

What makes the suppliers infallible?

Another line is: "Our store stands behind our merchandise." What does that mean? Get it in writing, shopper, and keep reading.

17. Haggling. While you are narrowing your choices to one or two pieces, you should be asking questions about prices and discounts. The tone of the discussion should be pleasant, even jovial at times. "Look, I'm not rich. I'm staying at the YMCA and washing dishes until I can find a flat. I'm buying this to cheer up my sick mother!" But be sure your clerk understands English well enough to appreciate the joke.

As for the YMCA reference, well, if they find out you are staying at the posh Peninsula or the Regent, do you think they'll give you the same discount?

It is sound thinking to believe that prices of goods near the source are lower than 3,000 miles away. For example, if a cloisonne pendant costs US$40 in your country, then you may be happy to pay $20 here without a fuss. But you *can* buy it for $10!

As a rule of thumb, tourists usually get 10-20 percent off without much effort, "just for you". This is to whet your appetite. "Residents" can get 30-40 percent off, more if you work at it or become a regular customer of some stores.

If the store discounts 60 percent in five minutes, then try for more. His first price is terribly inflated. When you look around, you will begin to know fair prices. In one rare shop, we found prices marked for tour groups. Learning that one of us was a local resident, the clerk cut the price in half, but it was still four times more than we could buy it for elsewhere.

The exception! When items are well priced, haggling does nothing but aggravate the situation. You must know when to desist. If you *must* have a discount as a matter of principle, try the "I'll-pay-with-a-credit-card" ploy, hoping for at least a discount for paying cash. It works unless you have thoroughly annoyed the salesperson and your purchase becomes unimportant to him.

Some stores selling mainly mainland Chinese products (see *Appendix*) have fixed prices but do give 10 percent discount "Courtesy" or "Privilege" cards. If you argue in person that you have just arrived and want to buy a lot of goods, they may give you a discount immediately. Try each department manager or the Overseas Chinese Service Department.

Even shops advertising "fixed prices" have been persuaded to come down a wee bit under unrelenting good-humoured pressure, especially when offered payment in cash.

Warning! We have only found one independent jewellery store that won't haggle. It has fixed prices marked in US dollars, a disadvantage for the local resident unable to benefit from currency swings.

So what's the best haggling technique?

(a) **Timing is important.** The best time for good buys is when fewer tourists are here and shopkeepers are desperate for cash flow — June, July, September, January to March, especially between the Western and lunar New Years. Chinese people must start the new year with no debts, and need cash to settle outstanding accounts. There are many sales during these periods, and discounts come more quickly.

If you are not in Hong Kong at these times, there's still hope. You may just happen to hit a time when the rent is due or a wedding is pressuring the family for cash. Some shopkeepers are superstitious about the first sale of the day, which is supposed to ensure good business for the whole day, just as the first sale of the new year brings good luck for the coming year.

Mornings are a good time for shopping. Business is sluggish, so you'll have more of the shopkeeper's time. Your chances of a "good deal" are better if there are no other customers around. The shopkeeper will not want to give the same big discount to the couple sitting down the counter eavesdropping on your negotiations. Prices punched on a calculator then replace the spoken word.

Avoid the 1:00 to 2:00 pm lunch hour. During this hour you will find newspaper-lined counter tops and heads buried in plastic lunch trays.

(b) **Deal with the manager if the purchase is major.** Store clerks can only discount up to a point, but the manager can go further.

(c) Say something like, "I would like this sapphire but you're asking $5,000. I was told Hong Kong prices are better. In Australia I can get a stone like this for $3,000. How about taking $2,000?" Point out that you probably want the shopkeeper to make a setting, and if the price is right you may want to buy three or four other pieces.

If he responds to your offer of $2,000 with an incredulous laugh, hold firm. The price of pride can be very high. He may counter your offer with 20 percent off or $4,000. Then it's your turn to laugh and make a "last" bid of $3,000, if that was your original goal.

Pleasantness is important here. Never get angry and raise your voice, for such behaviour is unacceptable here.

Dramatics are very important too. Pick up the stone, look at it again through the loupe, and if it's true, say "But it does have some scratches on it". For emphasis you may want to add with a grin, "Most people won't see it, but my mother will. She's a gemmologist".

At this point he may offer another gem for $3,000. If you want the first one, and you don't want to spend the day haggling, you might compromise at **$3,500** unless you can really get it for **$3,000** somewhere else.

(d) **Compare prices. It is customary here.** In fact, many stores have their business cards printed with a "memo space". Some even come with a map if you become lost in the jungle of shops and arcades. The other possibility is to get up and leave, saying that you saw a similar stone down the street and would like to recheck the quality or colour of that one. This gives you an easy exit from the shop and no one loses face if you do return and make the buy. If you do come back, try again for another few dollars off.

(e) **Don't give in to pressure tactics.** If a clerk is rude, *don't allow him to win.* He may be using such phrases as "You don't really want to buy, do you? You just want to look!" "I'm giving you a good price already" or "You don't trust me! You're hurting my feelings". Don't reward bad manners. Chances are there is nothing he has that can't be found elsewhere, so if you can't handle it, walk out with an "I need some time to think".

If he asks "How much do you want to pay?" give a fair answer. But be ready for this question, as you will hear it often. If you don't know what a fair price would be, say "Give me *your* best price and I'll consider it". Throw the ball back to him.

18. Get that detailed written receipt. You will need a receipt for Customs when returning home, and for insurance purposes. (See next chapter.) You will most certainly need the receipt if you later decide to return the goods or have your gems set into jewellery here.

Do you frequently change your mind after you buy things and try to exchange them? Be careful of this habit here. You are not in a large department store in Chicago or London where this is easily done.

The receipt must have the dealer's name and address, the type of stone ("natural Ceylon ruby", not "red stone"), origin, its carat size, dimensions (especially on large, expensive stones), colour (light or dark), any unusual characteristics, any damage or flaws, any treatment, gold content of the setting, and a clear statement of the return policy and time limitations.

Unscrupulous stores may accuse you of damaging or switching a stone should you bring it back.

If it is an expensive certificate diamond, over $30,000, be sure to collect the **certificate.** Not all diamonds merit trade lab certificates and the retailer must pay for them. They are an excellent marketing tool and a bit of security for the consumer who knows and understands them. Coloured stone certificates also exist.

19. Remember, when the store's policy allows for **exchanges for same value,** you must go through the whole bargaining process on the new piece. For this reason, *do not present the unwanted item until after the bargaining is over.* It may be a dirty trick, and in some cases unnecessary, but you are not at a disadvantage either. Bargaining might have stopped much sooner if they knew you would be exchanging.

Begin by relating back to the percentage discounted off the initial piece and try to apply this to the newly-selected one. Sounds simple but it may not be. You are not exchanging a shirt for a pair of slacks. You are attempting to exchange equal *value* for equal *value.* In jewellery, remember that mark-ups for diamonds, gold and so on can differ greatly. One thing is certain: all tickets have a bottom line and below that it is "no go".

If the store says you can get a refund or exchange in your home country at its branch store, be aware that there may be unforeseen complications. The branch may have had to pay duty on its goods, sales taxes, inventory taxes, higher salaries etc., all of which make its prices higher than Hong Kong's. Since you may not have to pay duty with your Customs exemption, nor do you usually calculate transportation in your costs, do not expect to get "equal value".

Some large, established stores may surprise you and give an even exchange, hoping the resulting goodwill will entice you back again — and it should.

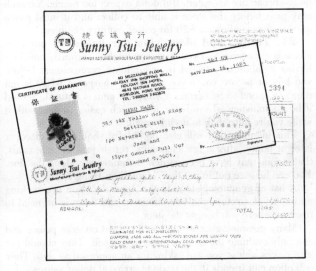

Samples of a typical certificate of guarantee and a receipt, bearing full particulars of the purchases.

20. Paying. The preferred form of payment is cash in Hong Kong dollars, and many stores will discount five percent if you don't use a credit card. Some may try to add three to five percent if you do use a card. This is not allowed unless you agree. Some stores prefer one card over another.

Traveller's cheques or cash in US dollars or other hard currencies are readily accepted. Just be sure you know the bank rate of exchange for the day.

Residents can usually use personal cheques drawn on local banks if presented with proper identification and a telephone number. Sometimes personal cheques drawn on your home bank abroad are accepted. But don't expect too much. A month may pass before the store is able to collect and it must pay a service charge of about $20 for out-of-country cheques.

21. Testing and identifying purchases. If your purchase is expensive and you have any doubts, seriously consider having it laboratory tested by a graduate gemmologist before you buy or before you leave. A testing charge of $150 is not much to spend to be certain a $35,000 gem is natural. Should it be a sophisticated synthetic, it is much easier to deal with it while you're here than to do it by mail.

This identification will also be helpful should you discover later at home, after a few cleanings, repair jobs or appraisals, that stones may have been switched somewhere along the line. You can be sure not to put the "blame" on Hong Kong.

A list of gemmologists is in the *Appendix*. You are seeking an impartial, professional identification and there is no need to disclose where you bought the item.

Many gemmologists are not well versed on gem prices and can only evaluate the quality of the gem itself. They should not give prices unless you are asking for an appraisal as well. They will often call friends in the trade to arrive at dollar values.

See also *Insurance and Appraisals, page 134.*

22. Returning your purchase. There may be many reasons why you want to return a purchase. (a) Your husband may not like his jade ring or he may think you spent too much for it. (b) You may suddenly discover you have spent more than you expected and can't pay your hotel bill. (c) You may have seen a similar gem at a cheaper price in another store. (d) You have merely changed your mind. (e) The store has deliberately or accidentally misrepresented the goods.

In any case, **first go back to the store where you**

bought it. If the store refuses to satisfy you and you feel it is at fault, then make a formal complaint to the Hong Kong Tourist Association or the Diamond Importers' Association. If the store is not a member, they will refer you to the Consumer Council. These associations should try to settle the problem as their literature suggests.

You should also inform the hotel concierge or whoever referred you to the store. He should know the full story and try to mediate as well. Many times it is a simple matter of communication. Or, in the case of "blowing your cool", a battle between two stubborn parties.

See also *Before You Buy Jewellery, page 109.*

Synthetic Gems and Imitations Seen in Hong Kong

Yes, there are synthetic and imitation gems on sale here, a few of these touted as genuine. Reliable stores will not misrepresent them. Some will not carry them at all to avoid mistakes and misunderstandings. Loose stone dealers might carry both, well labelled. At no other time in history have genuine stones come under such competition. It takes a true expert to identify them.

Imitations are just that: blue glass or plastic for aqua, bone for ivory, plastic-coated glass beads that look like pearls, cubic zirconium for diamond, etc. These are all considerably cheaper than the real thing.

Synthetics: These are man-made gems that duplicate nature almost to perfection. They are laboratory creations combining the same ingredients and conditions that nature took millions of years to create within the earth. Man has merely speeded up the necessary time to create them.

Cheap synthetics are the synthetic spinel and corundum produced by the Verneuil hydrothermal method. They take hours to create and emerge as large boules (cylinders) that are cut into hundreds of gemstones. They come in a variety of colours, and although they are chemically and physically almost identical to their natural counterparts, they can be separated. Definite identifying characteristics are seen through a microscope by trained experts.

The lay person will be most familiar with these synthetics in class rings and birthstone jewellery in low-karat gold mountings. In general their colours and transparency are too good to be true. Nature has a long way to go before being so perfect.

The high-priced sophisticated synthetics are a phenomenon of the 20th century and particularly the 60s and 70s. Practically all the major gems have now been duplicated by man but a few are not yet on the market. Some are too expensive to produce to compete with the natural stone such as diamonds. Many have natural looking inclusions and are sold in at least three qualities.

These synthetics are grown slowly in crystal form under strictly controlled conditions, duplicating and often improving on nature. At the time of writing, all of these can be tested and identified except for the quartzes.

The super synthetics were not created to replace natural stones but to increase market supply. All leave their factories properly labelled "Chatham-created" emeralds or rubies, or Gilson emeralds, opals, turquoise, lapis lazuli etc.

Unfortunately, some unscrupulous dealers are greedy and charge the same price as for natural stones.

Our personal feelings, which are shared by many in the gem trade, are that synthetics are a wonderful creation of man's technology, and that when properly represented to the public they have a real place alongside their expensive natural counterparts.

They have enabled the widowed grandmother who could never afford her birthstone to purchase a Chatham emerald and enjoy its beauty as if it were a natural. Once owned, a Chatham emerald would probably not be traded in for the real thing, as appreciation binds it to its owner.

Synthetic stones seen in Hong Kong are primarily rubies, emeralds and sapphires, but there are also a few amethysts, lapis and turquoise. Cubic zirconium is the most popular simulated diamond.

See also each gem section.

The Doctoring of Gems

Gem colours are influenced by metallic oxides and affected by extremes of heat and radiation. Nature usually takes millions of years to create some of its most beautiful colours this way. Man, however, has impatiently attempted to duplicate and hasten this process by heating stones or exposing them to gamma rays and electron beams. In many cases man has succeeded in increasing the supply of previously rare stones such as canary diamonds and azure-blue topazes.

There have been problems:

1. **A great deal of wastage.** Treatments are not always predictable. Some diamonds have turned brown rather than yellow with a consequent loss of value. Other stones shatter or become colourless.

2. **Some successes are only temporary;** e.g. irradiated precious topaz loses its colour within hours if exposed to sunlight and can only regain it by another dose of radiation.

3. **Careless handling** from Brazil has resulted in radioactive parcels of blue topaz that could be dangerous. Fortunately, none has been reported at the retail level and some were confiscated at a well-known wholesale gem show a few years ago.

4. **Coloured oil** has been added to jades, coral, pearls etc. The colour lasts from one to four years. More details in our section on each stone.

GEMS

An, gems! Over which wars have been fought, murders contemplated, lovers conquered and red tape endured!

Gems historically have been categorised as "precious" and "semi-precious", depending on their higher or lesser value. Rubies, emeralds, diamonds, pearls and sapphires were the most common "precious" gems, while topaz, aquamarine, tourmaline, garnet, citrine, amethyst, peridot etc. were considered "semi-precious".

Today this simplistic view of relative value is no longer used by gemmologists and up-to-date gem traders. These two terms serve no purpose and should be eliminated. For example, diamonds are listed as "precious" and may be bought for as much as $50,000 a carat or for as little as $2,000 a carat depending on quality. Garnets, previously classified as "semi-precious", can range from $6,000 a carat to $50 per carat. There isn't much precious about a $2,000-a-carat diamond except for the outdated impression of value. Do we call this quality level semi-precious? Is a $6,000-a-carat garnet expensive enough to be listed as precious? The categories are meaningless.

Most gems are inorganic minerals. Out of nearly 3,000 minerals, about 100 varieties can be classified as possible gem material. From these, only a handful are regularly set using precious metals to produce jewels. Out of these, only the ones most commonly seen in Hong Kong are described in detail. For this reason, there will be some obvious omissions for those of you who know your gems.

To be a gem a stone must have:

Hardness, the ability to resist scratching or abrasion. Hardness is not to be confused with toughness or tenacity, which is the resistance to breaking. The Mohs hardness scale *(Appendix)* classifies the relative hardness of substances from one to ten: talc to diamond. Diamond, the hardest of gems, is not very "tough" and may be shattered or chipped fairly easily because of its perfect cleavage. A hard stone is not necessarily a durable stone. Sapphire (9 hardness) has both durability and hardness. Jade is not particularly hard (6-7 hardness) but it is the toughest gemstone due to its interlocking crystal structure. (See Mohs scale on page 154.)

Rarity can refer to many things: unusual size and colour for a given species, deposit location, crystal form etc. Rose quartz as a mineral is common but crystallised rose quartz is extremely rare and that of faceting quality even rarer.

A rare gem will not achieve a high value without demand, and there must be a sufficient supply to create the initial demand; for example, andalusite is a borderline jewellery collectors' gem. A sudden burst of popularity would create demand and raise prices dramatically.

Colour or **hue** is the most important aspect of gem assessment. Usually the purer, darker and more intense the colour, the more valuable. What is *actually* the "best" is a matter of personal preference.

Clarity is the freedom from flaws, blemishes and visible inclusions. "Clean" gems may be common or extremely rare depending upon the species. Once only clean gems were considered worth buying even if the colour was good. Those with faults were shunned.

Today two things have changed this picture: fewer clean crystals are being found and some very good synthetics are on the market. Many buyers now prefer some inclusions in their gems as assurance of natural origin. A clean stone becomes suspect.

Transparency is the absence of inclusions in crystallised material. Without inclusions a gem can be said to be "crystal clear". With a profusion of inclusions, many gems become opaque or semi-translucent and their value greatly reduced.

Beauty, as with colour, is a matter of personal taste. The most beautiful quality is the rare combination within a species of top colour, clarity and cut. They command the highest prices and the market is always in short supply.

Portability is a factor that makes gems attractive to many people. They provide a high concentration of wealth in a small bundle. A fortune in fine gems can fit easily into your pocket, the lining of a suit, or a child's doll. Personally held gems can mean the difference between life and death in a political revolution, for example, where you are given little time to flee

STONE	SPECIFIC GRAVITY	.50 Ct	1 Ct	1.5 Ct	2 Ct
		DIAMETER IN MILLIMETRES			
Diamond	3.52	(5.2)	(6.5)	(7.4)	(8.2)
Cubic zirconia	5.70	(4.4)	(5.5)	(6.3)	(7.0)
Synthetic spinel	3.64	(5.1)	(6.4)	(7.3)	(8.1)
Corundum (ruby & sapphire)	4.00	(4.9)	(6.2)	(7.1)	(7.8)
Beryl (emerald)	2.72	(5.6)	(7.1)	(8.1)	(8.9)
Quartz	2.66	(5.7)	(7.1)	(8.2)	(9.0)

for your life. Refugees can begin again with a few valuable gems, as they are internationally recognised and valued. Gems and precious metals know no racial or international prejudices.

Every gem belongs to a mineral family or group. Within each family, members share the same physical characteristics such as crystal structure, hardness, specific gravity and refractive index. There are specific types of inclusions within each variety of gemstones.

But the colour within each family can be as vastly dissimilar as their names. For example, the corundum family encompasses both rubies and sapphires. Names might differ also according to country. Korea's "smoky topaz" is actually smoky quartz. No two gems are alike. Nature does not repeat herself.

How can you tell one gem species from another? Optical and physical properties are different in each. These variations must be studied using instruments such as refractometer, polariscope, spectroscope, microscope, ultraviolet light and heavy liquids.

A gem is properly identified by first eliminating what it is not. A casual look is only worth the experience level of the observer. Blue tourmalines shown to sapphire dealers in Thailand were met with, "Are these sapphires from Ceylon?" They had no idea they were tourmalines, as they had never seen them before.

The proper approach to "guessing" what a gem is without the use of instruments should be: "This blue stone looks like a sapphire or blue tourmaline, but I could be wrong."

How can you spot a glass imitation or synthetic? Read *Buying Techniques, page 21.* Consult also the test mentioned under each gem heading.

Your best selections in Hong Kong are the gems which the local Chinese themselves love: **emeralds, rubies, sapphires, diamonds, jade** and **pearls.** Hong Kong is also a very good place to buy **opals, ivory** and **coral.** Some local Chinese have opal interests in Australia and exercise first

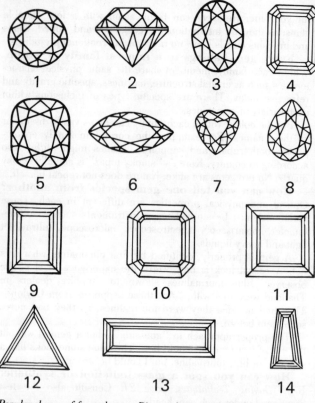

Popular shapes of faceted gems. Diamonds are usually cut 1 through 8, small diamonds 12, 13 and 14. 1. Top view standard brilliant; 2. Side view standard brilliant; 3. Oval; 4. Emerald; 5. Antique or cushion; 6. Marquise or navette; 7. Heart shape; 8. Pear shape; 9. Rectangle; 10. Square emerald cut; 11. Square cut; 12. Trilliant; 13. Baguette; 14. Tapered baguette.

choice of the production. Ivory has been worked in Hong Kong for many generations, and new jewellery designs surface yearly. Coral is abundant in many qualities, with much imported from neighbouring Taiwan. Fine cameos from Torre del Greco, Italy are also available (at Duty Free Shoppers).

A variety of gems are cut and polished here and then exported. **Citrines, amethysts, peridots, garnets, aquamarines** and **blue topaz** are primarily stocked for the tourist trade, and found mainly in Central and Tsim Sha Tsui.

AGATE and JASPER

Agate and jasper belong to the **quartz family** of gemstones and are known as **chalcedony.** They are *opaque to translucent* and come in colours and patterns which form a multitude of interesting varieties. They are hard, 6½ to 7 on the hardness scale, and are quite resistant to rough handling. They take a fine polish. They make into inexpensive jewellery items in cabochon or flat form and are also used for beads, carvings and art objects such as bowls, spheres, book-ends and boxes.

Agate carvings abound in Hong Kong, and value is placed upon the colours of the agate and how well the carver was able to incorporate these colours into the finished piece. Take time to examine a few of these carvings and see if you do not become entranced.

In Hong Kong, you are likely to see the following members of this group:

1. **Carnelian** or **Cornelian.** *Opaque and reddish-brown* variety which was once used for ancient seals because wax did not adhere to it. The red colour is enhanced by heat treatment. It was once thought to ease anger and quiet the blood. Chinese chops, both antique and new, can be found in this material locally.

2. **Chrysoprase.** The most prized of the chalcedonies is a lovely *translucent apple-green*, often mistaken for jade. Those

shoppers on a tight budget who fall for the finer qualities of jade would be wise to look into a piece of this inexpensive substitute.

3. **Bloodstone, plasma** or **heliotrope.** Take your pick of names for this attractive *dark green, nearly opaque* material with *red, iron-induced spots.* The ancients attributed the red spots to Christ's blood, and magical powers were attributed to it. Alternate birthstone for March.

4. **Enhydros** or **water agates.** These are *opaque to translucent* nodules of agate with water trapped inside. A polished window permits you to observe the water within. Very interesting water agate carvings may be seen at Lo and Rador's, and at the Chinese Arts and Crafts stores.

Over time the water may dry out. To restore it, place the agate in a basin of water for a day or so.

5. **Onyx** is actually black and white banded chalcedony, but most people think of it as *solid black.* Black onyx is dyed chalcedony and is popular and inexpensive.

6. **Moss agate** is very similar to dendritic quartz in that it shares similar tree-like landscapes and patterns of many colours caused by manganese, iron and chlorite. India is the best source. It is usually cut in cabochons, flats and beads.

Hong Kong is a good place to buy.

AMETHYST

Amethysts are the most expensive members of the **quartz** family and have been prized by royalty for their regal colour. The name comes from the Greek *amethustos* (not drunken), as it was believed to prevent inebriation.

Amethysts have a long history of popularity among the clergy and have frequently been used in rosaries and in the rings of bishops. No conclusive connections have been made between its sobriety claims and tippling clergymen.

It is said that amethysts vibrate love and are a medium

through which healing forces can be sent and received. They are best worn close to the heart and have a tranquillising influence. Amethyst is the birthstone for February.

Transparent

Colours: Like grape soda — from a light lavender to a deep rich purple which is often called "Siberian" when exhibiting a reddish flash. When too dark they lose their beauty and value.

Hardness: 7

Cuts: May be found in any shape but due to the natural crystal structure, large, round and emerald cuts are rare.

Geodes and fragments of geodes from Brazilian deposits are sometimes available here as specimens. These are very heavy and a traveller would be advised to visit a gem and mineral show in his home country to purchase one.

Sizes: From a few millimetres to 25-35 cts, the normal jewellery size being one to 10 cts.

If You Are Considering Buying

Most jewellery stores stock it as a popular February birthstone. Medium hues sell the best and are moderately priced.

Sources for Hong Kong: Brazil, Africa.

Ideal for any type of jewellery as it is tough and has no cleavage.

Fair price: $15 and up per carat for the lightest colours. The finest Siberian grade would be about $180 per carat.

Inspecting

Look for: Unattractive colour banding and colourless patches that detract from the overall beauty of the stone.

Inclusions: Few or none at all. But colour banding-zoning is often present and more easily detected when viewed from the bottom. With or without this zoning, the most important thing is how the gem "faces up", or looks when set.

Warnings

Imitations: Purple glass, fairly easy to spot with pronounced swirl marks and doughnut-shaped bubbles. Synthetic corundum is also made in a flat, uninteresting amethyst colour. The USSR is currently producing synthetic amethyst which to date cannot be differentiated from the natural. Both sell for the same price.

AQUAMARINE

Aquas, as they are sometimes called, are stones of peace and tranquillity. Their colour is said to be conducive to meditation. It is the birthstone for March.

Aquas are the blue variety of the **beryl family** and are found in large transparent crystals from which beautiful, flawless gems are cut. They are mined in many parts of the world but it was Brazil that made them popular. Brazil remains a major producer today.

Colour: Today the most observed colour is a pure sky blue, unlike the sea water colour for which it was originally named. Those greenish-blue hues are becoming difficult to find in the marketplace due to lack of popularity and demand, but they may become popular again as fashion changes.

The darkest blue aquas come close to sapphire blue, but this blue is rarely found in stones over five carat. On the other hand, the larger the stone the deeper the colour becomes. Small stones, however, rarely have sufficient colour to be attractive. The ideal size would tend to be five to 15 cts.

Hardness: $7\frac{1}{2}$

Cuts and shapes: Due to the large size of their hexagonal crystals, aquas may be cut into any shape. The most popular appears to be the mixed and step cuts. Rounds would be the rarest.

Sizes: Stones over 15-20 cts tend to be too large for conventional settings and may actually go down in price on a per carat basis unless the colour is exceptional.

If You Are Considering Buying

Most shops of any size have a few aquas. It is a popular

stone with Europeans and women who have fair complexions. Stones available here tend to be pale to medium blue, with few being well cut. Most show huge "windows" that allow you to read print through them. Little light is returned to your eye in the form of sparkle or brilliance. A badly cut aqua is not a pretty gem, and if you are to pay the price of an aqua it is advisable to get one that is well cut. Very dark ones are not readily available except through local wholesalers.

Sources for Hong Kong: India, Brazil and Africa. Possibly Burma.

Ideal for all types of jewellery. Anyone comfortable in light blue would appreciate an aqua. Especially good on blondes.

Fair price: $50-$150 a carat for the lowest colour range; $400-$1,000 for the highest.

Inspecting

Best lighting: 1) Natural daylight and 2) artificial light, ideal for evening wear. This may seem a contradiction, but if you *buy* an aqua under artificial light you might think that the colour you see is the true colour. But when you take it outside you will find that it appears much lighter. The important consideration is that you don't become disappointed with the lighter tone should you be buying your aqua for daytime as well as evening wear.

Look for: Well-proportioned stones without the see-through "window". There may be some inclusions, which should be noted on your receipt; e.g. "one partially-included aquamarine", etc. If your stone is flawless, it should be so noted.

Characteristic inclusions: Long straight tubes that can sometimes be seen with the naked eye but normally only through a microscope. There may also be flat inclusions that look like snowflakes. Flawless stones of good colour are becoming rare.

Warnings

Blue glass and synthetic spinel are the closest imitations. Garnet-topped doublets are also encountered from time to time. In general, aquas are a minor stone here in terms of volume and not subject to counterfeiting. Blue topaz provides a good substitute for expensive aqua.

The heat treatment of aquas has been going on for years to enhance their blue and "burn out" the green or yellow hue. This increases market supply and is a duplication of a natural process. The colour change is permanent.

Special Care

Aqua is a durable stone but it should be worn with the usual care given any fine piece of jewellery.

Frequent washing is advised as the light colour and high transparency show soap scum and dirt easily. Use ammonia and warm water or prepared jewellery cleaners.

CAT'S EYE CHRYSOBERYL or CAT'S EYE

Family: **Chrysoberyl.** Other varieties are alexandrite and transparent chrysoberyl. Beryllium aluminium oxide.

As its name suggests, cat's eye refers to a gem that displays a fine silvery-white line resembling a cat's pupil. This effect is produced by many fibrous inclusions aligned in parallel fashion which seem to blink open and shut, often with a bluish cast.

According to Richardson and Huett's book, this gem is supposed to have a slight stimulating effect on the adrenals. They suggest that you place a cat's eye on the navel for a few minutes as required. Try it and let us know if it works.

The name "cat's eye" in gemmology refers only to cat's eye chrysoberyl. All other cat's eyes must be designated by an additional name, such as tourmaline cat's eye or aquamarine cat's eye. The name should not be confused with the common quartz tiger's eye, which looks nothing like chrysoberyl.

Translucent

Colours: Pale greenish yellow, golden yellow to brownish yellow. The best exhibits the "milk and honey" effect when rotated.

Hardness: 8½. Very durable. Takes a fine polish.

Cuts: Only cabochons.

Sizes: Rare over two carat in fine quality.

If You Are Considering Buying

Seen fairly regularly in jewellery stores here because it is a favourite of Japanese tourists and other Orientals.

Sources for Hong Kong: Sri Lanka, Burma, Brazil, Rhodesia.

Frequently set in gypsy-type bezel mounting. Ideal for men's jewellery because of its durability and the masculine-type settings often used for cabochons.

Fair price: One of the rarest and most expensive coloured stones, cat's eye could easily cost $25,000 to $30,000 a carat in its finest qualities.

Inspecting

For best viewing hold about five or six inches under a concentrated light source. A penlight will do. The "eye" should be in the centre of the cabochon, not off to the side. Check for sharpness of the eye. The more compact the fibrous inclusions, the sharper and more definite the eye. Rotate the stone 360 degrees to get the blinking effect. One side of the eye is shaded, the other is light, hence the alternating milk and honey effect. Upon rotation, the line will "open" and "close".

Warnings

High quality synthetics are being produced, but so far we have not seen any.

Suggested Stores

Expensive larger stores like Shui Hing and Lane Crawford will often have a fine selection. Japanese department stores show a wider price range.

CITRINE

Family: **Quartz.** Citrine derives its name from an old French word, *citron*, meaning yellow. Most citrines found in nature are pale. Deep tones are rare. To increase supply, man has merely duplicated a natural process by heating amethyst and producing the various colours within this quartz variety.

Transparent

Colours: Light golden yellow to reddish brown. The most common is lemon yellow. The best colour depends on personal preference but the most expensive is a rich, reddish brown known as Rio Grande or Madeira made from very dark expensive amethyst.

Hardness: 7

Cuts and Shapes: All cuts available but cushion, pear-shaped and ovals are the most common. Large rounds and rectangular cuts like step or emerald cuts are more rare due to the natural crystal size and shape.

Sizes: Small sizes up to 25 cts, most commonly from one to 10 cts.

If You Are Considering Buying

Citrines found here are usually from India. Indian-cut stones tend to be bottom heavy and may sit too high off the finger when set into rings. Locally-cut stones are also available and may be slightly higher in price due to cutting costs. Rio Grande is not readily available locally.

Used for: Any type of jewellery.

Fair price: $15 a carat for very light, weak colours. The most expensive and rare burnt orange Rio Grande "Topaz" citrine can cost up to $150 a carat for stones over 10 cts.

Inspecting

Look for: The best are inclusion-free and without colour zoning.

Warnings

(a) Imitations are not a problem here as it is not an expensive stone. Glass could be used as a substitute. Synthetic corundum or spinel is sometimes used in birthstone jewellery as it is more durable, but it should be labelled as such.

(b) It can be confused with yellow beryl, topaz and tourmaline. These all look very much alike and the advantage is yours should one be substituted by mistake for citrine. These other stones are more valuable.

Special Care and Feeding

Ultrasonic cleaner can be used, but care should be taken if you clean with steam. No boiling. Heat sensitive.

CORAL

Calcium carbonate, with magnesium carbonate. This organic gem material comes from tiny marine animals that build reefs by secreting calcium carbonate to protect themselves. The calcified skeletons of their homes are what we use for jewellery. The best is grown in the warm waters of the Mediterranean Sea. It is grown very slowly, sometimes one inch in 18 months. It is getting very scarce as it is destroyed by polluted waters, suffocated by silt and dynamited by lazy fisherman.

Red coral was once used in medicines to build up blood, and traditionally has been worn as protection against evil and sorcery.

Unworked coral is dull but it has a fine vitreous lustre when polished.

Opaque

Colour: Range includes white, soft pink (angel's skin), orange, blue (Akori), dark red (ox blood), black (king's coral) and golden. The most valuable colour is generally the deep red, but fine pink angel's skin can be very costly as well. The more dense and even the colour, the better the quality.

Hardness: 3½. Brittle nature.

Available in great abundance in cabochons, beads and carved flowers, cameos and figures. Also used in clasps for pearls or other pendants. Some of the cabochons may be fluted into designs like Buddha heads for brooches or pendants and there are some very fine carvings made in Hong Kong, Taiwan and China.

Large coral branches are becoming difficult to find and

therefore the general sizes found on the market are average to small. Large brooches, pendants and carvings may be found made from old stock.

Some coral sold here is imported from Taiwan, where labour is cheaper and sources are local.

Pricing: Cabochons are sold by the piece, not weight.

Inspecting

Look for: Evenness of colour, freedom from blemishes, good polish etc. Look also for broken pieces and cracks that may have been glued back together.

Warning

Many imitations are on the market worldwide and a few may turn up in Hong Kong. These may be made of horn, bone, glass, plastic, stained calined bone, bonded coral dust or sealing wax.

Corals may be stained a deeper red or pink but a cotton swab dipped in acetone might remove some of this dye, leaving a telltale smudge on the cotton. If undetected, it could take three to five years before fading is noticed. Remember that many tests are destructive and only used as a last resort. They are better left in the hands of an expert.

Special Care and Feeding

Coral is very sensitive to heat and acids. Even the acids from the skin of the wearer can discolour it. To help maintain its original brilliance, only use a mild soap solution to clean it. Then dry thoroughly. See *Care and Protection of Jewellery.*

Care must always be taken to avoid breakage. Rings will need repolishing from time to time. As with all porous gem material, keep perfumes and cosmetics away.

DIAMOND

Diamonds have been a ruler's best friend for 6,000 years. They were first discovered in India; then in 1725 they were found in Brazil. Both these countries were overshadowed as world sources in 1870 when diamonds were discovered in South Africa. Today, leading producers are also found in Australia, USSR, Zaire, Angola, Ghana and South West Africa. It is the birthstone for April.

Diamonds have always been valued as precious stones, and in ancient times were used as both medicines and poisons. They were thought to darken if poisons were nearby. Some people considered them bad luck; others thought they brought good fortune.

Diamond prices are largely controlled by the Diamond Trading Co., owned by De Beers. The DTC limits the supply of rough diamonds sent to the Central Selling Organisation when prices are low, as in 1981-82. As demand overtakes supply, prices rise. A reported 80 percent of the world's diamond supply is controlled in this way.

Transparent: For jewellery use.

Hardness: 10. The hardest natural substance in the world. It can scratch everything. But it is not tough.

The Four C's should be considered when looking at diamonds. All four determine the price.

Carat: Since this is used for all gems, see *Glossary*. Flawless diamonds over one carat are now only two percent of all diamonds and are considered "investment" quality. The largest cut diamond we have seen on sale in Hong Kong was 20 ct.

Colour: Diamonds come in all colours. The "fancies" — blue, green, pink and yellow etc. — are very rare and expensive, with the colours faint. The more intense the colour, the higher the price. Stones of poor colour are subjected to atomic bombardment to produce pretty colours. Blue, green, yellow or brown stones are created and cost a fraction of the price of "fancy" natural diamonds.

Both natural and bombarded coloured diamonds are available in Hong Kong. Dabera specialises in them.

In addition to fancies, colourless diamonds are rare. These

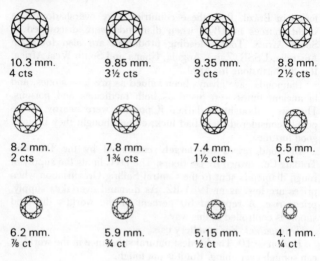

10.3 mm. 4 cts	9.85 mm. 3½ cts	9.35 mm. 3 cts	8.8 mm. 2½ cts
8.2 mm. 2 cts	7.8 mm. 1¾ cts	7.4 mm. 1½ cts	6.5 mm. 1 ct
6.2 mm. ⅞ ct	5.9 mm. ¾ ct	5.15 mm. ½ ct	4.1 mm. ¼ ct

Some brilliant-cut diamond sizes.

are graded in the chart opposite, the best "colour" being graded D by the much-used GIA system, and 100 by the Chinese. Ds are extremely rare, especially combined with a high clarity grade.

A stone's colour between an E and an H is usually indistinguishable to the naked, untrained eye but prices within this range can vary considerably. The price difference between a G and an H for a diamond slightly less than one carat, and about the same clarity, can be as much as $3,000.

For colour, always study a diamond against a matte white background in natural, north light, or under a cool-white fluorescent lamp.

COLOUR GRADING SCALE

Int'l Desig.	River (R)		Top Wesselton (TW)		Wesselton (W)	Top Crystal (TCR)		Crystal (CR)	Top Cape (TCA)	Cape (CA)	Light Yellow (LY)
GIA	D	E	F	G	H	I	J	K	L	M	N
Defin.	Colourless			Near colourless				Faint yellow			Very light yellow
H.K.	100	99	98-97+	97-96	95	94	93	92	91	90	89

CLARITY GRADING SCALE

	F	IF	VVS1	VVS2	VS1	VS2	SI1	SI2	P1	P2
Definition	Clean									
	Flawless	Internally flawless	Very very small inclusion(s)		Very small inclusion(s)		Small inclusions		Inclusions	
	Pure. No inclusion to be seen with a 10X magnifying glass		Very difficult to see with a 10X magnifying glass		Difficult to see with a 10X magnifying glass		Hardly visible with a watchmaker's eyeglass		Hardly visible with the naked eye	
H.K.	Clean		VVS	VS	1P	2P		3P	4P	LSP

Colour and clarity charts courtesy of Golay Buchel & Co. (HK) Ltd

See also *Settings, page 124.*

Clarity: A flawless diamond as defined by the US Federal Trade Commission is one with no "flaws, cracks, carbon, clouds or other blemishes" externally or internally when viewed through a 10X colour-corrected lens by a trained gemmologist. GIA's top clarity grades are F (Flawless), then IF (Internally Flawless) and VVSI (Very, Very Small Inclusions). Some dealers use the term "Pique" (PK). See chart on previous page.

Minute inclusions are not considered detrimental to the overall beauty or value of the stone if they are not black or in the centre. The setting will either cover or distract from them.

Inclusions cannot be seen by the naked eye in any stone VS2 or higher, so unless you expect your friends to attack your diamond with a magnifying glass, any grade in that range should do.

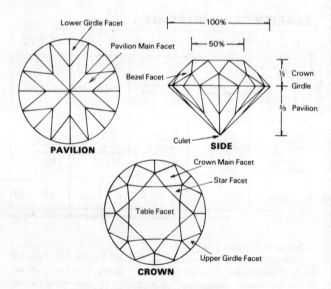

Brilliant cut showing ideal proportions.

Cut: The fire and brilliance of a diamond depends on the cut. The "fire" is the breaking up of white light into spectral colours. The standard "brilliant" (round) cut displays these qualities best. Emerald, oval, pear and marquise cuts look bigger for their weight per carat but are not as bright as the standard brilliant. The new 144-facet, round "constellation" is expensive and not always available. The "radiant" is an improvement on the emerald cut. In a "brilliant" cut diamond, the distance from the table (the top) to the girdle (the widest part) should be about one-third of the stone.

See also section on *Gems* in general.

If You Are Considering Buying

You can expect lower prices in Hong Kong because there are no import taxes and lower mark-ups. World prices in early 1983 were starting to go up after being very low for a couple of years. There is usually a correlation between high inflation and high diamond demand, and high interest rates and low diamond demand.

Whether you decide to buy a one-carat flawless diamond of poor colour or a top colourless diamond slightly flawed is a matter of personal preference and cost. Somewhere between the colour and clarity grades and combinations of the two, there is just the diamond for you.

Certificates

Most diamonds here are graded by gemmologists using master sets of comparison diamonds. Many stores also carry diamonds graded in the US for one carat and larger. Only diamonds graded by the GIA in Santa Monica or New York City are allowed to carry GIA certificates. The price for a certificate diamond compared to a similar diamond which is not graded by the GIA is an additional one to 15 percent. Make sure you get the right certificate for the diamond you are buying.

Ideal for: All kinds of jewellery.

Warning

Diamonds do chip. Care should always be taken when you wear them, especially if they protrude above the setting. A bezel setting offers the most protection but not the best display.

Diamond imitations are many, but all of them can be scratched by a real diamond except for a diamond-topped doublet. The most popular, abundant and successful diamond imitator is **cubic zirconium,** known as "cubic" or CZ, and most are sold as such, "Russian diamonds" or "Gemarons".

Many CZs are set in silver and are very reasonably priced. We recommend them for a young girl's first "diamond" studs. Why take a chance that Tammy will lose a real diamond when she can have the same look for a fraction of the price? This also takes the pressure off Tammy should she lose one.

If your husband bought you a CZ, you would probably be insulted. However, if you bought yourself one and it passed among your friends for a diamond, you would be elated because of the successful joke.

CZs are very inexpensive, selling in 1984 for as little as $42 a carat depending on where they were cut. They come in at least six colours, but we feel only the pink looks believable as an imitator. The other colours are too intense.

We recommend the use of small CZs in place of diamonds to show off a larger, fine coloured stone if you cannot afford both the good stone and the diamonds. This is a wise thing to do while in Hong Kong because of the lower setting costs. When you have more money or another anniversary, have the CZs replaced with real diamonds. This can be done by mail if you can't come back to Hong Kong, either by sending back your ring or ordering the same-sized diamonds.

Sending your ring back and paying the duty when it is returned will probably be cheaper than having the work done in America, Australia or Europe.

The most fraudulent practice involving CZs is their use as side stones instead of diamonds. Larger stones are not much of a problem in Hong Kong. The smaller the CZ, the more difficult it is to detect with the naked eye. Many stores are also concerned that they will purchase a diamond melee salted with CZs and inadvertently pass them on to their customers. For this reason they might test these purchases with a portable testing machine that detects CZs through thermal conductivity.

NOTE: Be aware also of a diamond doublet with a diamond crown and a CZ pavilion. The girdle texture is different.

Special Care and Feeding

Can be cleaned with an ultrasonic cleaner and hot liquids, household ammonia and detergent.

Suggested Stores

All jewellery stores carry diamonds. For "fancies", both colour and shape, try Lane Crawford, Shui Hing, Casey, Manning, Dabera, De Silva and Golay Buchel.

For natural diamond crystals set in imported French jewellery, try Casey Boutique.

For stones one carat and larger try King Fook, Shui Hing, the jewellery stores in the Landmark or the Peninsula Hotel, De Silva, Dabera.

For CZs in silver try Men's Jewellery Centre.

For unset CZs try Lo and Rador.

Diamond Design Competition

Every year for the last eleven years, the Diamond Importers' Association has organised a competition for the best diamond jewellery designs. Entries have come from Southeast Asia, China and Hong Kong.

You may want the prestige of owning some jewellery designed by one of the winners of this very important contest. In Hong Kong, the companies and stores with winning designers in the 1983 competition were:

Chow Tai Fook Jewellery Co.

Tse Sui Leun Jewellery

Lloyds Jewellery

Chow Durk Yu Trading Co.

Diamond is Forever Ltd
Gosachi Jewellery Designers
Casey Diamonds.

EMERALD

Family: **Beryl.** Aluminium beryllium silicate. Emeralds are the rarest and most valued member of this family, worn by popes rather than cardinals or bishops. They have been prized since ancient times in Egypt, India, Greece, Rome and among the Aztecs and Incas. Staring at an emerald was said to improve the eyes. It is also associated with love, and was believed to fade when exposed to evil. Emerald is the birthstone for April.

The green colour is derived from traces of metallic oxides, chromium and vanadium. Some purists label only beryls coloured by chromium as true emeralds. Vanadium-coloured green beryls are usually much lighter in colour. Spectroscope examination will separate the two.

Emeralds, unlike other beryls, are found in small crystals.

Clarity: "Clean" stones are extremely rare. No emerald is entirely free of inclusions, but magnification may be required to locate them. Only the finest qualities are completely transparent. Emeralds with too many inclusions tend to be somewhat cloudy and dull.

Colour: Light green, yellow green, blue green, dark blackish green, to fine emerald green which many authorities feel is incomparable in its finest hue. The closest any other gem comes to this colour is Imperial jade. The most valued colour is a dark, intense green without a hint of blue or yellow, but this is a matter of taste. The highest prices are always on the purest green tones.

Hardness: 7½ to 8

Cuts and shapes: Usually "emerald cut". This is a square or rectangle, many times found with the corners cut off to lessen the chance of breakage. The sides are step cut, which shows off the stone to its best advantage. Any cut may be encountered but due to the high cost of the rough and the hexagonal crystal structure, the emerald cut is the most economical. Fine cabochons are also available and are less costly than faceted stones. Carved emeralds, generally from India, are made from flawed material of good colour.

Sizes: Vary from a few millimetres used for side stones or bands, to 20 cts or more. The average size is from ¼ ct, or 25 pts, to one ct.

If you Are Considering Buying

Hong Kong has a profusion of emeralds with an unusually large supply of big stones. World emerald supplies are strong and prices are good locally. It is an excellent time to buy.

Sources for Hong Kong: Worldwide, especially Africa, Brazil, Colombia, India etc. Historically Colombian stones were considered the best, and you may pay a premium for them. However, unless you are an expert and carry a microscope, you will not recognise a Colombian from a Zambian. Stones should be judged on their own merits and not by their source.

Used for all types of jewellery. Generally found set with diamonds which enhance their beauty and colour and lend some protection against damage. Yellow gold mountings complement emeralds.

Not recommended for men's ring stones because of fragility. Try an equally nice synthetic Gilson or Chatham instead. Should it break, the financial loss will not be great. Chatham stones are replaceable free.

Inspecting

Look for: The most valued is a combination of fine colour and high crystallisation with a minimum of inclusions. An inclusion-free emerald over one carat is however a matter of "legend". Consider first your colour preference, but if an emerald just looks like a green stone with no life or personality, give it some more thought. There are many less expensive green patches of colour that would do equally as well.

Look also for stones that are not too thin or flat, for these may break easily.

There are usually plenty of inclusions which are to be expected and endured. The major consideration is that they are centred within the stone and do not reach out to any surfaces. Your fingernail can usually detect any coming to the surface, which can lead to a broken stone.

Warnings

(a) Misrepresentation is usually in the form of doublets or triplets. Mostly seen by jewellers in old pieces, some may have a garnet top with a green glass base. The garnet fuses readily with the glass and the seam is polished smooth. Another fake may consist of two pieces of colourless quartz or beryl glued together with green cement. The stone when tested with a refractometer will give an emerald reading. There have also been cases of green glass giving the same readings as beryl.

(b) Synthetic emeralds produced by Chathams and Gilsons are available locally. They are beautiful and reasonably priced.

(c) Be aware of the universal practice of oiling emeralds. This is done to eliminate the visibility of fractures, thus increasing brilliance. Also used occasionally are coloured wax and plastics.

A problem arises if dye is added to the oil. With time, the oil dries out and leaves a concentration of colour along the fractures while the stone pales. The stone can be re-treated, but chances are that you undoubtedly overpaid for this "fine" (artificially improved) colour.

(d) Glass imitations.

(e) It is possible to confuse emerald in its many shades of green with chrome diopside, tsavolite garnet, chrome tourmaline and Imperial jade.

See also *Synthetics and Imitations, page 39* and *Buying Techniques, page 21*, especially about certificates.

More Warnings

Since emeralds generally have many inclusions and possible

fractures that can weaken the durability of the stone, they must be worn with care. A sharp blow could break the stone along one of these fractures. The closing of the prongs while setting or during repairs could also damage them.

Special Care and Feeding

No ultrasonic cleaner or heat. Brush gently with warm, mild soap solution.

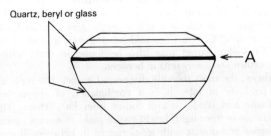

Quartz, beryl or glass

←—A

"Emerald" triplet. "A" is green cement.

GARNET

Within the large garnet group there are six species and twelve varieties that differ widely from each other chemically but share the same crystal structure. All colours of the spectrum except blue are possible to the lucky person with the January birthdate.

The ancients ground garnets into powder and drank the potion to relieve fever and treat jaundice. It was a gem worn to signify faith and truth and was once used for bullets both in Asia and by the North American Indians.

Transparent to translucent

Colours: The rarest are pure orange and emerald green. Because of the wide range of colours, varieties and prices, garnets make a most desirable gemstone.

Almandite or **almandine** is probably the best-known variety in jewellery and is a dark red with possible purple overtones, $20 a carat and up. It can also be found in star form resembling star corundum.

Andradite provides a variety, **demantoid,** which is a rich, green gem found only in small sizes. Mostly seen as small side stones in antique pieces.

Grossularite has two varieties, **hessonite** and **tsavolite.** Hessonite, or cinnamon stone, is a rare yellowish brown similar to fine topaz. Tsavolite is a rich emerald green, in its finest qualities making a perfect emerald substitute for a tenth of the price. Grossular garnet may also be found in pink, white, yellow, brown and many tints in between.

Malaya, the most recently discovered garnet, has received much publicity of late. It is a combination of spessartite, grossularite and rhodolite and comes from East Africa. The colour range is from light, bright pastel pinks to orange, going into intense red-orange with tonal ranges in between. It may also exhibit a changing of colours like alexandrite. The price is high and commensurate with its rarity and beauty — US$250 to $1,000 a carat.

Pyrope is the reddest variety and the most easily confused with ruby. When of average quality, pyrope is very much like almandite. Without specific tests it is impossible to separate the two.

Rhodolite is one of the brightest and prettiest of the reddish-purple garnets. It exhibits a high degree of translucency. A combination of almandite and pyrope, it can resemble the plum colour of sapphire. Ten-carat sizes are available, but the price jumps considerably. Normally one to five carats.

Spessartite's colours range from yellow-orange to orange-red with brown overtones. It may be confused with hessonite in some qualities. In its pure orange colour it is quite rare, especially if "clean".

Uvarovite is another beautiful green garnet only found in tiny crystals, and rarely seen unless in antique pieces.

Hardness: $6\frac{1}{2}$ to $7\frac{1}{2}$

Cuts and Shapes. With the transparent varieties: step, mixed and brilliant cuts. For the translucent stones, cabochons look best.

Sizes: The majority of garnets are small (0.25 cts to five cts). A few species may be found over 10 cts, primarily rhodolite.

If You Are Considering Buying

Garnets are abundant locally and may be found in a number of varieties: rhodolite, tsavolite, almandite, hessonite and malaya. The one hitch is that a clerk may not know what kind they are. You will have to rely on the colour definitions we give as a guide.

Main sources for Hong Kong: South Africa, Brazil and India.

Ideal for: All types of jewellery. Indian garnet beads are plentiful and inexpensive.

Look for: Purity and richness of colour, freedom from flaws and good polish. Avoid overly dark stones and loose stones that are chipped. Check garnets set in jewellery for nicks and abraded facet edges.

Inclusions: A large, clean, inclusion-free garnet, like a clean emerald, is rare.

Warning

There is more likelihood of confusing garnets with other gems than of finding outright fraud. Some garnets are close seconds to the colours of sapphires, rubies, emeralds, peridot, zircon and possibly spinels.

Special Care and Feeding

Garnets tend to be somewhat brittle. The abrasion level is greater than with many of the harder gems and thus they may need to be repolished more frequently. Always remember that flawed stones should be excluded from ultrasonic baths.

GOLDSTONE

Aventurine Glass. This commonly seen gem material is man-made glass. Goldstone is most often a reddish-brown colour exhibiting a pretty, spangly effect. This is caused by masses of thin, triangular or hexagonal copper plates interspersed with the glass. A goldstone is also produced with a blue ground.

Large carvings and inexpensive jewellery from this material are frequently seen in shops here. Few shopkeepers are aware of its true nature and will be put out if you suggest it is not a natural gemstone.

IVORY

(Note: the *Asian* elephant, whale and several other animals are on the endangered species list and importation of their by-products is forbidden in many countries. These are not allowed to be sold in Hong Kong, but you may come across the odd piece in stores. The ivory of the Asian elephant has a whiter and denser texture than the African. It is easier for craftsmen to work but it yellows more quickly.

(See *Customs Regulations* in the *Appendix, page 139*, before you consider buying any ivory.)

Ivory has been worked since ancient times in Egypt, Assyria, Babylon, Greece, Japan, India and China. King Solomon had an ivory (and gold) throne. Because of its long tradition in China, the art of ivory carving here is also highly developed.

Dentine from elephant, hippopotamus, walrus, narwhal, boar (warthog) and two different types of whales are considered forms of ivory. In this section we primarily look at the tusks of the African elephant, which is not currently considered endangered, and is the source of an estimated 95 percent of the ivory sold here.

A tusk is a tooth. The average tusk weighs 15-16 lbs, but a

tusk can be anything up to 200 lbs and 10 ft long, of which half is hollow. It is easy to cut. Shopkeepers here talk of "soft" (or "Cape") ivory, or "hard" ivory. These terms refer more to sources in Africa and how difficult it is to work. Both ivories are within the 2 to 3 hardness range. The "hard" ivory is more difficult to cut and will take a good polish, whereas the "soft" ivory is more resistant to extremes of temperature and will not crack as readily due to its porous nature.

Ivory is composed of calcium phosphate and has a greasy to dull lustre. Depending on which part of the tusk it was cut from, it can be either *somewhat translucent* or *opaque*.

Colour: It is found white or creamy in nature, but when "antiqued" with the help of tea, shoe polish or smoke, it closely resembles genuine antique ivory, which is yellow or brown.

If You Are Considering Buying

Hong Kong is an ideal place to buy ivory because its Customs control on endangered species is internationally recognised. You should not have much hassle with Customs in other countries over ivory purchases made here. Local carvers are more familiar with Chinese themes, but can also carve to order.

From the outside most ivory stores look alike, many with a large, very detailed, ornate, pieced-together dragon boat, chess sets, balls within balls within balls, sculptures, brightly painted ladies and Chinese cabbages with grasshoppers. The jewellery includes necklaces, brooches, rings and bracelets.

Upon closer inspection you will see differences in quality of carving, subject matter and style. A few will have European themes. You may think you have found an original but be assured that if that "original" sells well it will be copied by other stores very quickly. If you have an original design made up, at least you can say you have a first edition.

Inspecting

Look for: 1. Grain. While some imitations have some graining, they do not have the distinctive "engine turning" lines only associated with elephant ivory. These are fine, crossed, parallel lines visible to the naked eye. However, you may or may not see any grain depending on what part of the tusk the piece was carved from.

2. In large, solid pieces, look for the nerve hole running through the centre of the piece.

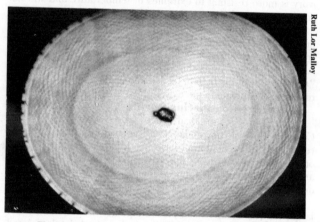

Elephant ivory — engine turning showing central nerve.

3. Cracks or breaks.
4. Brown staining to give a new piece the look of an antique.
5. Colours. Many pieces here are painted, a process that is permanent and does not adversely affect the value. Painting is a matter of taste and at one time all ivory was painted. The Japanese are especially good with colours, and these pieces can sometimes be bought locally but are more expensive.

Warnings

1. Imitations are of celluloid (plastic), which does have some

similar marks but not graining. A moulded imitation is frequently revealed by the seam where the two halves of the moulds join. Celluloid is slightly softer than ivory and less dense.

These imitations, some made partly with bone dust, are found in souvenir shops, open markets and alleys. They are mainly in the form of *neksuke* Japanese-style carvings of a little over an inch up to statues of 12 inches or more. They make an excellent, cheap, lightweight souvenir as they range up from $4 in the alleys and look very oriental.

A *netsuke* is an ornamental figure originally used to attach a purse or any other article to the sash of a *kimono*. You will find balls inside balls inside balls in plastic as well as ivory. They are considerably cheaper and have been assembled.

2. Bone. This is the best ivory imitator, slightly more expensive than plastic. There is nothing undesirable about this imitation except the deception, particularly if you have to pay the higher ivory prices. A good place to study the difference is in a Chinese products store which sells both, well labelled.

Bone carving does not have a high polish or lustre. It has no graining, but tiny holes. It is lighter in weight than ivory and more porous. Bone carvings should give you no problems with Customs unless they are from whalebone. Carvings here are usually bovine or camel.

The quality of workmanship on bone can be just as good as on ivory. The alleys in Tsim Sha Tsui are filled with bone and plastic carvings of all types.

3. Fake antiquing. (See above.) Very few genuine antique ivory pieces are around. Look for concentrations of colour along grooves and creases for the fakes. Also note the lines. Old tools left lines less sharp than the dental tools used now for carving.

Special Care and Feeding

Some people may feel that ivory is a good investment because of possible future shortages or embargoes. The US had such an embargo a few years ago. An investment is well and good if you have the proper storage conditions and wish to take the risk.

1. Ivory is subject to cracking with extremes of temperature and humidity. It should be kept in a relatively humid environment. Notice that a small glass of water is in each shop window.

2. Clean with a damp cloth and polish dry. Anything else should be done professionally. Avoid cosmetics. Because of its porous and absorbent nature, ivory can absorb oils from the skin which will wear off the high polish and finish.

While in Hong Kong, we suggest you take in any ivory pieces you have for cleaning, polishing and repairs to any ivory shops. Don't attempt to polish out scratches or stains yourself. Expertise is needed. This service is much less expensive here than in most other places in the world.

If you do not have your pieces here, take damaged pieces to any expert lapidary at home.

3. As with all organic gems, ivory should not be kept in plastic bags. It needs air to "breathe".

Other Ivories Available Here

We have found that if you ask for anything but elephant ivory, the clerk is immediately defensive and suspicious of your intentions. Maybe he fears that you could be checking for the Agriculture and Fisheries Department for some forbidden merchandise.

Hippopotamus: These tusks look like miniature elephant tusks. Generally they are a yellowish cream and are frequently carved with a scene. Small individual teeth may also be made into snuff bottles or carved into flowers or *netsuke*. Hippo ivory is more dense than elephant and thus harder to work. But the price is about the same as elephant ivory.

Molars: You may find a tooth (molar) from a hippo or elephant nicely polished, carved or engraved with a scrimshaw design by noted Hong Kong artists Yue Shan or An Yuet Shan.

Look for their signatures. Their work is generally in the old whaling tradition and depicts scenes from the life of the North American whaler.

As there are also sperm whales' teeth (endangered species) available, we urge you to consider *Customs Regulations, page 139*. Some of these teeth are left over from Japanese fishing expeditions and are polished and mounted on rosewood stands and also graced with scrimshaw.

Suggested Stores

A concentration of three or four ivory factory/stores are in the Wyndham and Wellington streets area in Central behind the Chinese Arts and Crafts store on Queen's Road. There are also many shops in the Tsim Sha Tsui area.

A few stores act as retail outlets for four to six factories. You must buy in volume (usually ten or more) to get the ex-factory prices. Some stores have carvers on the premises and may allow you to watch work in progress. If you don't want to leave a demonstration to chance, contact the store in advance and make arrangements. The Tack Wing Ivory Factory told us this could be done.

JADE

This term is applied internationally to both **jadeite** and **nephrite.** However, the Chinese use it for many other hard stones as well. For example, they are not necessarily trying to deceive you when they tell you serpentine is "new jade". Often they don't know the difference.

Jade for the Chinese has traditionally been a very special stone. It symbolises the five cardinal virtues — wisdom, justice, charity, courage and modesty. It means beauty, nobility and purity. They believe it changes to better colours if the personality and health of the person wearing it are good.

At the same time this magical stone, which they say fell from heaven, protects the health and fortunes of the wearer. In Hong

Kong you will see little babies wearing bracelets or pendants of jade. The ancient Chinese also believed it slowed down the decomposition of the body, and in recent years 2,000-year-old corpses have been exhibited covered in complete suits made of nephrite. The body openings of corpses were also plugged with jade to keep evil spirits from entering, with a carved cicada generally found in the mouth. At one time famous pieces of jade were traded for whole cities.

Partly because of this strong traditional attachment and its proximity to Burmese sources, Hong Kong is the world's leading jade trading centre. In 1982 it exported more than $51 million worth of jade and jade jewellery.

Nephrite and jadeite are not related except in appearance, and this may cause a big problem with identification. Nephrite is a silicate of calcium and magnesium, and jadeite is a silicate of sodium and aluminium. They have different refractive indexes. Nephrite tends to be more opaque, but in both cases the more translucent, the more valuable. Nephrite is tougher. It takes 50 tons of pressure to crush a one-inch cube. It is the toughest gemstone in the world.

Nephrite

Dates back to the Shang dynasty more than 3,000 years ago, when the ancient Chinese worked a tough, green mineral which they called *yu*, a name still given to any hard green stone. It has been used for centuries for tools, weapons and ritual ornaments not only by the Chinese but many other cultures, including the American Indian and the Maoris of New Zealand.

A type of nephrite, sometimes known as "mutton fat" because of its colour and oily appearance, is very special, particularly to the Chinese.

Hardness: $6\frac{1}{2}$

If You Are Considering Buying

It is usually seen in "old pieces". The jade market is filled with it, called "old jade", a name applied also to a much softer soapstone imitation. Because of nephrite's interaction with minerals in the ground, it is often buried with dead animals and later dug up hoping for beautiful alterations in colour and texture that would make it more valuable.

The main cutting centres today are Guangzhou, Beijing and Hong Kong. The main source for the rough is Canada and the US. When store clerks tell you a stone is from China, they mean the stone was cut there and usually have no idea of its source. "Chinese jade" is probably nephrite.

Jadeite

More beautiful than nephrite because of its colours and lustre. It was discovered in the 1800s in upper Burma, the world's only important commercial source. Every February, at the Burmese Government's annual trade fair, boulders of rough jade are sold, the quality within unknown. "Windows" are "mawed" into each boulder for a peek. The stakes are high and fortunes have been made or lost as each buyer hopes for a vein of rich Imperial green jadeite hidden within the crusty, weathered skin.

Colours: Jadeite is purer in tone, and more extensive in range. You should find yellow, mauve, blue, violet, black, orange, red, brown, pink and white as well as many shades of green — spinach, apple, and the most highly prized emerald or Imperial green.

Seen under magnification, jadeite has a dimpled surface, somewhat like orange peel.

Hardness: 7

For Both Nephrite and Jadeite

Cuts or shapes: Mainly cabochons and small carvings for pendants, clasps and brooches. Carvings of ornamental and religious subjects.

Look for: Translucency and evenness of colour and texture. In opaque jade, good colour and texture is more desirable than dull coloured translucency. In jadeite carvings, the more colours in one piece the more valuable it is, especially if the different colours have been cleverly worked into the design. Because jade is such a hard, tough stone to carve, the more intricate and fine the work, the more valuable.

A large 12-inch carving might take six months to three years to render. The quality of the carvings from China is usually better than those done in Hong Kong.

Sizes: Jadeite pieces are usually smaller than nephrite, and jadeite is not so frequently found in large carvings.

If You Are Considering Buying

Jadeite has only been worked in China for the last 150 years. Anything offered as "antique" jadeite from the early Ching dynasty cannot possibly be authentic.

Fair price: Check out prices and quality at any China products store and use these prices for your guideline.

Warning

There's a lot of dyeing going on with green and lavender jadeite. The colour will last one to three years only. It defies the acetone test, but can be detected by laboratory testing.

During the late 1950s a jadeite triplet came into the marketplace with the colouring of Imperial jade. The triplet was made up of (1) a hollow cabochon, a very fine translucent white jadeite, (2) a cabochon of a smaller size made of the same white jadeite, cut to fit into the hollowed-out section of the upper cabochon, and (3) a flattish, oval piece fashioned to close in the back. The centre cabochon is coloured with a jelly-like dye of Imperial green colour. The dyed centrepiece is inserted into the hollowed cabochon and the bottom piece cemented on, repolished to make a perfect fit and to help eliminate the seam that is caused by joining.

When unset, the nature of this triplet is readily seen from the join and outer pieces. If set with the edge concealed in a bezel, you should have reason to be suspicious. A gemmologist can check with a spectroscope, and sometimes you might be able to see a bubble in the jelly-like dye under magnification.

"Jade trees," forests of which seem to grow in every China

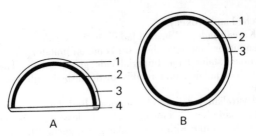

Jade triplet. (A) Side view and (B) top view. (1) consists of green, jellylike glue. (2), (3) and (4) are translucent white jade. The glue can usually be seen under direct light.

products store and curio shop, are mostly of quartz, jaspers, agates and serpentine. Prices are reasonable for these and the "jade fruit". Real jade would be much more expensive.

The Hair Test: Some clerks will wrap human hair around a piece of jade and then attempt to burn it. When it doesn't burn, they announce that the stone is genuine jade. Don't be taken in. This test proves nothing.

Imitations: Many are on the market. Jade can be easily confused with many other stones commonly seen around Hong Kong.

Jade tests (Destructive tests not recommended)
1. Steel razor blade or penknife does not scratch surface.
2. Industrial steel file will scratch it.
3. For triplets, try the water test. (See *Buying Techniques.*)

Imitations
Prehnite
Aventurine
Chrysoprase
Serpentine or bowenite
Verdite
Soapstone (steatite) (hardness 1 to 1½. Can be easily

scratched and broken).

"Korean jade," "Suzhou jade" or "new jade" are actually serpentine or bowenite, the most common imitators. These are sometimes stained the Imperial jade green colour. They are softer than jadeite, and readily distinguished with a spectroscope.

"Australian jade" is chrysoprase; Red Jade is carnelian. "Honan jade" or "Nanyang jade" is less than 10 percent jadeite. It is white with rectangular green spots. "Indian jade" is aventurine (green quartz).

LAPIS LAZULI or LAPIS

Family: **Sodalite.** Lapis is made up mainly of three minerals: lazurite (blue), pyrite (yellow) and calcite (white). It was worked by the ancient Egyptians, Hindus and early Buddhists, and at one time was considered just as precious as gold. Ground up into powder, it has been used for cosmetics, medicines and paints (ultramarine). Students of Egyptology may recall that it was found in King Tut's tomb.

Opaque

Colour: Deep royal blue, tending towards violet in the finest qualities. Some people prefer to have the brassy yellow pyrite showing. It is a matter of taste. The purist prefers the more expensive evenness of colour.

Hardness: $5\frac{1}{2}$ to 6

Found in all types of jewellery. Generally seen in cabochon form but may be carved or smooth. In polished flats it is worked into beautiful inlay designs with other materials. Lapis is fashion-conscious and slips in and out of popularity. Currently it is slipping. It is well suited for men's jewellery because of its rich blue colour, providing a masculine and tailored look.

It takes an excellent polish and is also used for carvings and ornamental objects.

If You Are Considering Buying

Hong Kong is a good place because of old reserves from Afghanistan and a continuing supply coming from Pakistan — the two best sources. There is also a fine Soviet deposit. Chile produces a lower grade which has more calcite showing. It is used primarily in carvings. Due to the war in Afghanistan, there's a dwindling amount on the world market and prices have been rising.

Fair price: It is sold by the piece here, whereas elsewhere it is sold by the carat. Six or seven-millimetre round beads in fine quality can be $2,000 to $3,000 a strand. Six-millimetre earring studs with 14K backs sell for $200 to $250.

Special Care and Feeding

Do not use an ultrasonic cleaner. Care should be taken as it is easily scratched and may need repolishing.

Warnings

The cheaper, more abundant sodalite can be dyed to look almost identical to lapis. The dye can be detected by rubbing a piece of cotton wool dipped in acetone (nail polish remover) over the piece and observing a blue dye residue on the wool.

Be suspicious if the price is too low, as lapis has never been considered inexpensive.

It can also be confused with azurite, lazurlite, sodalite and glass imitations. Gilson is producing some very nice synthetic lapis with pyrite inclusions which cannot be detected.

Suggested Stores in Hong Kong

Sunny Tsui, stores specialising in Chinese products, and Lo and Rador.

MALACHITE

This decorative stone is an ancient gem material used in 4000 BC by the Egyptians. Centuries ago it was considered a magical stone and used for healing, or as protection against disease, the occult and lightning. It is formed from dissolving copper ores.

Opaque

Colour: Always green, from light to emerald to blackish green, usually with banding or stripes. A skilled craftsman takes advantage of these beautiful markings and works them into a desired piece.

Hardness: 3½ to 4 and fairly easy to break, especially along the graining.

Used popularly as flats for inlays. Hong Kong is filled with malachite carvings, everything from Buddhas to horses to beauties. It is also lovely in beads, cabochons and in designer jewellery for men and women. It continues to be a popular stone due to its beautiful colour, easy workability and fine polish.

Along with lapis, malachite jewellery tends to come in and out of fashion. Currently it is waning.

If You Are Considering Buying

Hong Kong is a cutting centre for malachite and is a good place to buy.

Sources: Africa (Zaire) is the main source. Beautiful material comes from Russia and the quality of workmanship from there is unsurpassed.

Pricing: Sold by the piece, not carat weight. A cabochon for a lady's ring should cost $35 to $50.

Inspecting

Look for cabochons with good proportions and polish with a pretty design or pattern in your choice of green. The higher qualities are less porous, stronger and without much banding.

Special Care and Feeding

Because it is easily scratched, we would hesitate buying a malachite bangle or bracelet for everyday wear. It can be easily repolished, however. It is brittle and tends to break if dropped. Crazy glue works wonders mending broken pieces together almost invisibly.

OPAL

Family: **Silica group.** This October birthstone is the most prized of the silica group. It is also the most rare when it exhibits the wonderful "play of colour" for which it is famous. Without this display, the mineral itself is as common as its cousins quartz and agate. It is not crystalline like the other two, but is amorphous without crystal form. It is usually found in small pieces from which doublets and triplets are commonly made. A cap, generally made of quartz, protects the thin seam of usually black opal. Doublets are highly recommended for ring stones.

At one time during the 1800s, opal was considered unlucky partly because of the role it played in Sir Walter Scott's novel

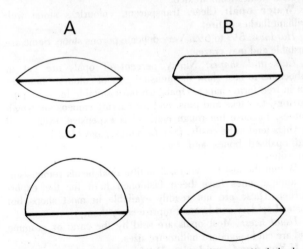

Opal doublets. All tops are precious opal. Bottoms are (A) chalcedony, (B) glass, (C) opal matrix and (D) common opal.

Anne of Geierstein. In the Orient it is a symbol of hope and fidelity.

Colours vary according to the type of opal and include every colour in the rainbow.

White opal: Opaque, the most familiar, with fine multi-coloured flecks and flashes of colour on a light base. It often needs a dark backing to highlight the colours.

Black opal: Has a fine play of colour on a dark translucent background of black, green, blue or grey, orange and violet. It is the rarest and most costly of opals, reaching into $10,000 per carat. The most valuable shows reds and oranges.

Fire opal: Transparent to translucent with an orange-red to red body colour. It may or may not show a play of colours or fire, but it is more valuable if it does. It is lovely, and may be faceted. Comes from Mexico.

Water opal: Clear, transparent, colourless stone with brilliant flashes of fire.

Hardness: 5½ to 6½. Very delicate porous stone. Some are unstable and may craze.

Cuts and shapes: Ninety percent of opals are cut in cabochons to best show the unusual play of colours. Some are cut in free form shapes. Opals are most suitable for pendants, earrings, tie tacks and pins, and for carving cameos and small statues. Because the rough material is expensive, even small carvings tend to be costly. (See *Carvings, page 116*.) Fossilised and opalised bones and shells are sometimes available as curiosities.

Within the last few years, beautiful opal beads reminiscent of antique ones have been fashioned here for the export market. These are not readily available in most shops but Luster Lapidary and Lyons Emprise carry them.

Usual sizes: Most opals are sold by the carat or gramme and are cut in standard millimetre sizes.

If You Are Considering Buying

Precious opal is readily available. Hong Kong is the major

cutting centre for Australian rough, and prices are lower here than in Australia.

Warnings

Care should be taken when wearing opals, especially in rings. Opals are frequently set surrounded by diamonds as much for beauty as for protection from severe knocks. They can be chipped.

Opals are porous and contain water. Do not expose them to extremes of temperature, hand cream or detergents — they may discolour or crack.

Some lovely synthetics are being produced by Gilson. Both whites and blacks are available in two qualities and cost considerably less than natural ones.

Inspecting

Hold the opal under a good light and tilt it in all directions looking for the play of colour with each new position. The more play and variety of colour, the better the quality. Light opals should be observed and mounted on a dark background which will enhance the fine colours.

Special Care and Feeding

Opals contain from 10 to 30 percent water. They tend to dehydrate over time. As a result they may craze and lose much of their beauty. An occasional soak of a day or so in water will help restore lost moisture.

Do not store them in plastic bags.

A soft, clean cloth should be used gently to wipe opals free of dirt. Opals are not for every day. Common dust particles are made of quartz crystals which, when rubbed into opals, will scratch them. It is not difficult for a lapidary to repolish abraded opals, especially cabochons.

PEARL

The Queen of Gems has been cherished as a gift from the sea for more than 5,000 years. Roman women even wore pearls to bed to remind themselves of their personal wealth upon awakening. There was a time when only European royalty was permitted their use along with silver and gold. Pearls reached such a height of popularity at one time that one period in history was known as the Age of Pearls.

Of interest to collectors might be the carpet of pearls that was $10\frac{1}{2} \times 6$ ft and once valued at several million US dollars. It was part of a vast collection of natural pearls kept in the royal treasury of the Gaekwar of Baroda in India.

Although the Chinese cultured pearls in the 13th century, it has not been until modern times that man has improved on nature by culturing pearls to perfection. No longer left to chance, the world's supply of pearls is now assured, and the royal gem of history may be treasured by all. It is the birthstone for June.

This section is limited to cultured pearls, as the natural "oriental" ones are rarely encountered and are prohibitively expensive.

CULTURED PEARLS

Pearls are created when man places an irritant within the body of a mollusc or pearl oyster. This irritant is called the nucleus. The mollusc begins secreting concentric layers of nacre around this nucleus for up to seven years, the most productive period being from three to seven. With each additional year the risks of imperfections are increased. Only 10 percent of all cultured pearls grown are of fine quality.

The size and ultimate shape of the pearl is dependent upon the growing time, the size of the mollusc and the type of nucleus. The nuclei may be beads of mother-of-pearl, soap-stone, shell or plastic, either round or cut in half. For freshwater pearls, a tiny piece of tissue from another mollusc's mantle is inserted to stimulate pearl formation.

For an excellent step-by-step display, we suggest a visit to

Golay Buchel in Central. (See *Appendix, page 145.*)

Pearl evaluation

In addition to size, the GIA lists five factors to consider when grading pearls. Keep them in mind while looking for your strand. The difficult part of comparing prices and qualities from store to store is remembering them. If you want to buy ten strands of freshwater pearls, for example, buy one of the colour and quality you like from a store that has several. Take that strand with you to compare qualities in other shops to see if you can do better elsewhere. If you see something you prefer, the comparison pearls can be sold or given away as a gift.

Look for:

1. *Colour.* Most pearls have had some type of "colour adjustment" made to them after harvesting. This is not of great concern unless the string or drill holes are stained with dye indicating that the colour is unstable.

Terms associated with pearl colour are:

(a) BODY COLOUR, the overall, predominant colour of the pearls. It may be light (white, pink or cream), black (black, dark grey, bronze or dark blue, or with metallic overtones) or coloured (those which fit neither of the above categories and are mostly freshwater pearls). "Coloured" are best seen in soft-diffused light.

(b) OVERTONES are the additional colours reflecting more from the surface of the pearl. These may be rosé, blue and green. You may encounter a pink-rosé, which means a pink body colour and rose overtones. The most valuable combinations are pink, pink-rosé and white-rosé.

(c) ORIENT is the rarest of the three and is another word for iridescence. Only fine, thickly-coated pearls with thin and transparent nacre platelets will display this rare quality.

Pure, even colour is most desired in pearls. The best quality natural pearl colour is primarily a matter of taste. Currently pink is fashionable, and goes well with fair-skinned people. Cream-coloured pearls go well with brunettes, white with

Orientals. Also popular are greys, blues, blacks and lavender. Yellow to golden tones are the least desired in this part of the world.

Well-dyed or irradiated black pearls with metallic green overtones are as costly as fine natural colours. Blue, grey or silver often are less expensive than the blacks.

2. *Lustre:* The reflection of light from the pearl's surface can range from mirror-like to dull. High lustre should also have even intensity.

3. *Nacre thickness*

Very thick	over ½ mm.	best
Thick	½ mm.	good
Thin	¼ mm.	passable
Very thin	less than ¼ mm.	poor

The thickness of the nacre not only affects the beauty of the pearl but also its durability, the thicker the better. A poor quality pearl with a thin nacre of less than ¼ mm. will "blink"; i.e. its lustre will be uneven, and it will look mottled, as if it had peeled in spots.

You might be able to see the thickness of the nacre through the drill hole. Or under a fluorescent light on a white or grey background you can see two concentric circles on the pearl. The inner circle is the nucleus, the outer the nacre. You could have pearls X-rayed by a dentist!

A natural pearl will be almost all nacre; a cultured pearl almost all nucleus.

4. *Roundness:* The more round the pearl, the higher the value and rarity. Money may be saved by choosing a slightly "off-round" shape unnoticeable at three or four feet. In order of quality, we have the spherical, off-round or out-of-round, semi-baroque and baroque. The semi-baroque and baroques are the best buys here as you can attain large sizes with high lustre at very good prices.

5. *Texture:* Refers to blemishes like scratches, cracks,

bumps, discolorations or an uneven surface or "skin".

6. *Sizes:* Usually measured in millimetres. Irregularly-shaped pearls are measured by their second widest proportions or by their two largest dimensions.

Round salt-water pearls range in size from 1 mm. to 10 mm. with most in the 5 to 8 mm. range. The most popular size is 7 mm. to 7½ mm. The larger are generally the more costly.

The grading of pearls is more complicated than grading diamonds. What you buy in Hong Kong will undoubtedly receive a very high evaluation in your home country providing you follow these guidelines. Check out the pearl experience level of your home jeweller before showing him yours. Pearl prices have increased so rapidly that unless a jeweller has been buying regularly, he will tend to evaluate your purchase based upon old price sheets or faded memory.

Varieties of Cultured Pearls

1. **Blister** or **Mabe** (pronounced ma-bay). A large ½ bead is planted on the inside shell of the mollusc. When harvested later, it is cut directly from the shell, the bead removed, replaced with a mother-of-pearl bead and set in a closed back as a pin, ring, brooch, pendant or as earrings. This form of pearl is not particularly strong and there is no way to know how thick the coating is. If set in a ring, care is required. If broken, replacement in the exact size may be difficult.

2. **Biwa** (bee-wah). Although originally from Japan's Lake Biwa, these are now a classification of fine, freshwater non-nucleated pearls. They are seeded with mantle tissue from various freshwater mussels with up to forty planted at one time in each large clam. The growing time is three years and the clam may be used again for a new harvest. Average size is 3 to 6 mm. with fine surface texture, lustre and colour. Many interesting shapes can be created as well as a wide variety of natural colours. China and other countries are now producing freshwater pearls with many rivalling those of Japan. However, on the whole these are more wrinkled in skin texture and lack

the uniformity in all areas that exemplify the classic Biwa.

3. **South Sea** denotes location. They are cultured in very large molluscs and average 11-12 mm. Rarely do round ones reach 14 mm., but irregular shapes may be this large. The most prized colour in the whites is the silver-pink and in the blacks the peacock-green.

In May 1983, two strands of thirty-nine South Sea pearls sold for $200,000 and $270,000 at a Sotheby auction in Hong Kong. Each pearl measured about 10×15 mm. South Sea pearls are today's queen, with the newly-cultured Tahiti blacks king!

4. **Black** are cultivated in the black-lip oyster in Tahiti and the Gulf of Mexico. These naturally black pearls are extremely rare and expensive and will not generally be seen here. Most black pearls are dyed, and some of these can be costly depending on the quality of the pre-dyed pearls. Poorly treated ones will fade or rub off on your clothes. The most valued black pearls have a metallic finish with green overtones. Cultured black pearls range from 3 to 8 mm. Any size may be dyed.

Selecting your Pearls

Now that you have read the guidelines for selecting the best, let's pick yours. First of all, set a budget and aim for the best within that budget. Regardless of what others may deem the "best" colour, you choose what you like and *what looks best* on you. The salesman will want to sell you the pink rosé, but if you like yellow pearls buy some and save money over the whites. Sure you deserve the best, but in this case the best might not be the most expensive!

Do not become intimidated. Don't worry if one or two pearls are a bit "off". They can always be put to the back of the necklace or omitted completely.

Prices: In terms of relative costs, the most expensive pearls are natural pearls, then South Sea, then large Japanese rounds and semi-baroque. Cheapest are Chinese freshwater pearls.

Rounds: For 8 mm. and larger, the price jumps dramatically. However, there have been years when 5-6 mms were quite rare because demand outstripped production. A glut of 7s and 8s once made prices higher for 5s and 6s. It's a matter of supply and demand.

Special Care and Feeding

Yes, be careful. Don't use anything harsher than mild, non-detergent soapy solution or a commercial pearl cleaner like the one Hagerty puts out. It may still be available at Evergreen and Lane Crawford here. Dip, rinse and dry well on a flat surface. Never hang up to dry as the string may stretch out of shape. Never use an ultrasonic cleaner.

There should be knots between pearls which keep the pearls from abrading one another and wearing down the drill holes. They also assure you of only losing one pearl should the string break while you are running across a busy street.

Keep your pearls away from other jewellery that may rub against them, and store in silk bags or a box, never in a plastic bag. Pearls need to breathe and should not be put away in a vault where, with time, they will dry out and turn yellow.

All cosmetics, perfumes and hairspray are poisons to pearls. They destroy the fine lustre and eat into the nacreous coating. Tying long ropes of pearls into knots is not a good idea. It causes them to wear against one another unnecessarily. Try a pearl shortener to adjust length or put two clasps on a long strand to provide for variations of use.

Pearls should be restrung at least every two years. Dirt gets into the drill holes and forms an abrasive action causing the nylon string to break. Most breaks occur near the clasp, where they are usually handled.

Warnings

Imitations: Clues to heed — unknotted necklace of perfectly matching beads (size, colour and texture) coupled with a cheap clasp, usually of silver.

A simple but not foolproof test is to rub a pearl up and down against your front teeth. It should have a gritty, uneven feel. Most imitations will slip and move smoothly across your teeth. Some can feel gritty. Practice this at home with known imitations and natural pearls. If you continue to suspect the strand, stick a pin into the pearl's surface. A coated imitation pearl will become scratched or indented. The natural or cultured pearl will not.

Most of the imitations are sold in the alleys or street stalls, but remain alert even in shops.

Add a Pearl: In the US some jewellers market "add a pearl" necklaces for "your little girl". You buy one pearl at a time for a special occasion. We do not advise this practice. You will pay too much and will end up with an unmatched strand of pearls.

See also *Customs Regulations* and our section on *Beads, page 111,* especially about clasps, bead sizes, strand lengths, knots and counting beads before and after you surrender them to be restrung.

PERIDOT

Magnesium iron silicate. *Mineral species:* **Olivine.** This August birthstone, which is also known as olivine and chrysolite, has been mined on St John's Island (Zebirget) in the Red Sea for almost four thousand years. It was thought to be divine and was once believed to glow in the dark, ward off spells and have special healing properties for the spirit. In any case, its lack of "fire" does give it an aura of serenity. It has been found in meteorites and in association with volcanoes.

Transparent

Colour: Sleepy-looking olive or yellowish-green, much like the colour of new leaves. The most desirable shows no brown or yellow.

Hardness: 6 to 7

Cuts: Found in oval, round, brilliant and mixed cuts.

Sizes: Generally small, one to five carats. Over 50 ct and flawless are now rare. The Smithsonian in Washington, D.C. has a 319 ct stone.

If You Are Considering Buying

As with all the other coloured stones not popular with local Chinese, peridot is encountered only occasionally here for birthstones. It is relatively inexpensive when under 10 cts.

Sources for Hong Kong: Mainly the US and Burma.

Ideal for brooches, pendants and earrings, but not for bracelets and rings because they are easily abraded. Looks best set in yellow gold.

Inspecting

Look for double refraction. Inclusions and back facets are seen as two. Peridot has an oily vitreous lustre.

Warning

Glass, synthetic corundum and synthetic spinel imitations are made. While these will probably not be found in Hong Kong, it is always wise to look for spherical bubbles or compare a known gem with the suspect for a warmer temperature indicating glass.

The synthetic spinel is much cheaper, harder, and will wear better for active people who want the peridot look without the care.

Special Care and Feeding

Fragile stone. Wear with care. Will need repolishing if worn frequently in rings. Brush with mild soap solution, no heat. Ultrasonic cleaners will cause stones with inclusions to break.

QUARTZ

Silicon dioxide. The quartz group is the most common and varied of all and found worldwide. There are two categories: macrocrystalline and microcrystalline (or cryptocrystalline). In this section we will deal with the macrocrystalline varieties. See *Agate* section for microcrystalline.

In antiquity all yellow stones were called topaz, and this practice continues today with much quartz being sold as "golden topaz". In the US the Federal Trade Commission has ruled that such quartz must be so labelled as in smoky "topaz" quartz.

Modern-day wizards have applied quartz's electrical powers to radios, phonographs, lenses and watches. Much of this industrial demand is filled with synthetic quartz from Russia and Brazil.

Quartz is an interesting collector's stone. It is inexpensive, colourful, and may be found with over forty different included materials. Some of these make very beautiful gemstones and carvings.

Hardness: 7

The following have been seen in Hong Kong:

1. **Tourmalinated quartz.** Clear quartz with black (schorl) tourmaline crystals throughout. It may have a few crystals or be heavily impregnated with them. This makes a very handsome stone, faceted as beads, or carved.

2. **Dendritic quartz** has inclusions that look like fine black and white branches of miniature ferns produced by manganese oxide. When iron is present, the branches are brown and gold. The branches are not fossilised plant life, though they may appear so.

Dendritic quartz is often confused with Indian moss agate. It is recommended for jewellery and interesting specimens.

3. **Rutilated quartz** is also known as "Venus hair stone". This has fine red or golden rutile needles, much like hair, throughout. Brazil is a major source, and it is seen here in snuff bottles, chops and carvings.

4. **Aventurine** is usually a green rock containing mica. Sometimes a special form of mica, called fushite, acts as the green colouring agent and produces a beautiful sheen that sparkles in the light. India is the major source, and beads and carvings abound in Hong Kong.

5. **Tiger's eye** and **Hawk's eye** are very popular opaque materials from South Africa. Colours may be brownish-yellow in tiger's eye to bluish-green in hawk's eye. The tiger's eye can be bleached a honey colour or dyed an artificial-looking red or green. The quartz fibres inside give a shimmering effect of chatoyancy to the stone. These fibres were once asbestos.

The material is seen everywhere in Hong Kong and is very inexpensive. As with most cabochons and flats, it is sold by the piece and not by carat weight. It is used mainly in rings, beads and small carvings for pendants, statues, boxes etc.

6. **Rose quartz,** as the name implies, is found in a strong pink to almost white colour and is cloudy with many fractures. Rarely is it crystallised and transparent enough to be faceted. It is used primarily as a carving medium, frequently as flowers, and is very popular in the Orient. Beads and cabochons are also available and combine nicely with amethyst. A faceted stone is considered unusual but not expensive. The best colour is medium dark pink.

7. **Smoky quartz** "topaz" is undoubtedly one of the best-known gemstones and is particularly striking when expertly cut. Its colours range from a light to dark brown with a smoky tinge. The darkest brown is called "morion".

The colouring is believed to be produced by natural radiation within the earth. Upon heating, lighter shades are produced in some stones or total discoloration in others.

We usually see this material in faceted gems and carvings. It is so inexpensive that a silver, gold-plated mounting should be considered instead of karat gold. A $50 stone in an $800 setting is silly. Smoky quartz is under $10 per carat.

8. **Rock crystal** at its finest is colourless and transparent. It was so named by ancient Greek mountain climbers who thought it was frozen water. Roman ladies fondled small spheres to cool their hands. In the Middle Ages sorcerers gazed into crystal balls much like some modern-day seers.

A word of caution to fortune-tellers seeking a new crystal

ball. Many on the market are made of glass which will have swirl lines, gas bubbles and will be warmer to the touch than natural crystalline gem material. Any rock crystal balls found over three inches in diameter without inclusions are rare.

RUBY

Family: **Corundum.** Rubies are perhaps the grandest of gems, and are in constant battle with emeralds for the exalted position of the most costly. They have an aura of mystery and symbolise love and courage.

The Hindus once thought that colourless sapphires were "unripened" rubies and reburied them in the earth to ripen into fine red gems. Those found with many flaws were considered "overripe". It is the birthstone for July.

Opaque to transparent

Colour: Corundum, which is too light a red to be called ruby, is properly called pink sapphire. A definite red is necessary to justify the name "ruby", and this is not generally adhered to in Hong Kong. In fact, when asking for a pink star sapphire recently we were met with looks of confusion. Pink star "ruby", yes. About 80 percent of the shops continue to label all corundum of the red family as ruby regardless of how light it may be.

Hardness: 9, second to diamond's 10. Very tough and extremely durable, a wonderful gemstone for all types of jewellery for men and women.

Cuts and shapes: All shapes may be encountered but the majority are in mixed cuts with rounds, cushions and ovals predominating. Cabochons are also popular. Paler stones tend to have intentionally deep pavilions to darken the colour. This also adds excess weight.

Sizes: In general rubies are small, 0.25 to one carat, but some are up to five carats. Fine stones over five carats are rare and costly. We suggest several small stones set in clusters to give the effect of one large, much more expensive ruby.

Large gem quality stones are rare and some antique pieces once thought to be ruby were later identified as natural red spinel. Fine star rubies over three carats are scarce.

If You Are Considering Buying

Hong Kong has an abundance of rubies for sale from many sources in all price ranges. Examine the subtle differences of colour and decide what you like for the price you can afford. Rubies are shown on yellow gem papers and look best in yellow gold.

Sources for Hong Kong: Burma, Thailand, Sri Lanka and Africa.

Burma has the reputation of producing the finest. Top grades from other sources are also sold as "Burmese". Do not be intimidated into thinking that because a jeweller says his ruby is "Burmese", it should have a higher price tag than one from Thailand. The quality, not the origin, is the factor here, particularly when virtually no rubies are coming from Burmese deposits today.

They should be a dark "pigeon's blood" red to cherry colour, without being overly dark or light.

Stones from Thailand and Cambodia tend to be dark with purple or brownish-red overtones similar to garnets. They are much cheaper.

Stones from Sri Lanka tend to be lighter in colour than those from Burma and of purplish to pink tints. They tend to be more brilliant than those from other sources and less severe in colour.

Look for the best colour for you, taking into consideration the relative pricing structure for each category (Burmese, Thai etc.), evenness of colour with a minimum of the colour zoning common in the corundum family, freedom from internal and external blemishes, pleasing cut or shape, and a fine bright polish.

For judging "stars", see the last section in *Sapphires*.

Warning

Ruby is undoubtedly the most difficult and most frequently tested stone in Hong Kong. The characteristic inclusions found in a synthetic are very natural looking and only trained experts can differentiate between the two. There have been a few cases where synthetics have slipped through the labs here graded as naturals, only to be re-evaluated by the GIA in the US as synthetic.

Garnet and glass doublet imitations are also on the market here and look beautiful in settings. If loose or prong-set, try the immersion test to be sure. See *Synthetics, page 39*.

SAPPHIRE

Family: **Corundum.** The name comes from a Latin word meaning blue, and like its red sister, the ruby, it comes with an illustrious history and an association with royalty and high clergy. It was worn by bishops, and the British crown jewels contain many famous stones. It is the September birthstone. It was thought to have curative powers for many ailments, to attract poisons and other impurities and to keep its owner safe.

Translucent in cabochons and stars, and transparent in faceted form. Much of the blue sapphire today is heated or "burned" to dissolve the silk-like inclusions and lighten and clear up the stones.

Colour: The names of countries have become quality designators but these qualities are not necessarily from these countries. The "best" colour approaches violet blue of a medium dark tone. The word "sapphire" always means blue unless preceded by another colour qualifying it, such as "pink sapphire".

Trouble can occur in distinguishing between the pinks and reds. At what point does a deep pink become a ruby? Most fancies come from Sri Lanka and are gaining in popularity.

The most highly prized and costly of the fancy colours is the natural orange-red padparadscha, a Sinhalese word meaning "lotus flower". Fine Imperial topaz is its closest rival.

"Australia" — dark, inky blue stones with heavy colour zoning, the best of the greens and pretty greenish-yellows.

"Burmese" — Mogok Stone Tract is the source of fine royal blue gems that look best in natural light and lose some of their brightness at night. They may have a slight violet hint.

"Ceylon" — light blue, bluish-grey, yellow, violet, white, green and pinks. Much of this material is parti-coloured, more than one colour in the same stone. The blue zone must be oriented just right in cutting to flood the stone with colour in order to make it saleable. This often results in irregularly shaped stones that are difficult to set.

"Kashmir" — "cornflower-blue" gems that have a subtle, hazy, almost velvety lustre. This quality looks best for dinner rings under artificial lights.

"African" — widespread occurrences throughout South and East Africa in all colours.

"Thai" — indicates very dark bluish-black, of the lowest grade to US dealers and a high one quality below top Kashmir to the London merchants. However, there are many fine gems from Thailand. In Hong Kong a fine Thai stone may be called Burmese to increase the price. Be observant. What's in a name? Judge the stone for itself.

Hardness: 9, just under diamond (10). Very tough and takes a fine polish.

Cuts and shapes: Mostly mixed cuts, the same as ruby.

Sizes: Similar to ruby in commercial jewellery sizes. Large stones are more prevalent than large rubies and more affordable. With increased size, however, prices per carat do escalate.

If You are Considering Buying

Fine small and large gems are available along with the inexpensive dark, navy blues that Americans and Europeans tend to recognise. Take another look before you buy and see if you don't actually prefer the more medium hue. Hold the ring or stone at arm's length. Is it blue or black? If blue, you are heading in the right direction. The blackish ones are worth $60 or less a carat, considerably less than the blue. You pay much more when this black quality is incorporated into a setting than you would buying the stones alone. Price it out if you don't believe us.

Ideal for: All types of jewellery for men and women. It wears very well and suits everyone because of the myriad of colours to choose from. Always looks nice with diamonds.

Best lighting: Look at it under both artificial light and daylight and decide if you want a day stone or an evening stone. Remember, Kashmir sapphires are evening gems.

Look for: Evenness of colour, freedom from flaws that will affect beauty or durability, and a fine polish. Never forget for a moment to note the overall cut and proportions of the stone.

Inclusions: Very specific inclusions do occur that synthetics have not duplicated — *yet.*

Warning

The golden colours on the market over the past few years have been irradiated and the colour may be unstable, much like the Imperial topazes. Should it fade and you want it restored, you could try to find a jeweller to radiate it again. This, however, may be difficult.

Be sure to get a certificate or guarantee that the stone's colour is permanent.

Synthetic sapphire has been with us for a long time and in many colours. It is generally produced to imitate other gems, mainly as birthstones and in class rings, and not as natural sapphire.

Natural blue spinel or tanzanite may be passed off as more expensive sapphire, and they are also lovely stones. In years past, garnet-topped doublets were common, but they are much less common today.

Special Care and Feeding

Due to its hardness and toughness, a sapphire should withstand years of use. As proof of this, note that many engagement rings have a diamond flanked by sapphires, a custom especially popular among the British.

Stars — both rubies and sapphires

Star gems, like cat's eyes, are called phenomenal stones and are truly a wonder. They have captivated the imagination of gem lovers for centuries. Both are cut in cabochons to release the eye or star.

When judging stars: All the criteria deemed necessary for evaluating transparent corundum is also necessary for the stars. In addition we add proportions. With the cabochon star, there should not be more than one quarter of the total weight below the girdle line. Beyond that, you are paying for extra weight that adds nothing to the beauty of the gem.

The more translucent, while still exhibiting a clear star, the more valuable. All six of the intersecting rays should be as close to the centre as possible and not off to the side. The rays should appear from deep within the stone and not radiate from the surface as do the old synthetic Linde stars.

Examine stars under a single direct overhead light source. Be aware of trade tricks done to improve stars. The unpolished rough backs of star gems may be rubbed with a lead pencil intensifying the effect of the star. Wax and oil, to name a few, are often added to conceal cracks and imperfections. Both of these practices are temporary and thus fraudulent. Microscopic examination and cleaning are methods for detection. Always insist that any treatments be disclosed on your receipt so that you can be prepared for any alterations.

SODALITE

Sodium aluminium silicate. Sodalite is a component of lapis

lazuli and is similar in appearance. Rarely does it crystallise.

Opaque

Colours: Deep shades of blue, interspersed with white calcite and occasionally with yellow pyrite specks. Most valuable is a rich, almost navy, blue with a minimum of white.

Hardness: 5½ to 6

Used for: Most types of jewellery in cabochons, beads and flats. Also used for carvings and ornamental objects like boxes, spheres and ashtrays.

If You Are Considering Buying

Sodalite is seen more frequently as art objects.

Sources for Hong Kong: Brazil, India, US and Canada.

Ideal for all kinds of jewellery but is overshadowed by the richer coloured lapis lazuli.

Moderately priced in its finest grades, a poor man's lapis.

Inspecting

Look for dark even colour without calcite specks.

Warning:

Sodalite may be confused with lapis lazuli when pyrite is present along with calcite, but the blue colours are very different. It has no violet hue. It is usually full of calcite. The safest way for a gemmologist to differentiate the two would be a specific gravity test. Actually, you would be the lucky one mistakenly to buy a lapis article for the price of sodalite.

Sodalite may also be dyed to cover the calcite. This can be detected by the acetone test described under *Lapis lazuli*.

TOPAZ

This stone was revered by the ancient Egyptians because they associated its yellow colour with their sun god. Since then, at various times in history, it was believed to give strength, to act as a protector, to cure blindness and to make its wearer invisible in emergencies. Like some other gems, it was supposed to warn people when poisons were near by changing colour. It was also ground up and used as a medicine.

There are many colours to choose from for the November birthstone, so be on the lookout if you don't like yellow but want a topaz.

Transparent

Colours: In its purest form, it is colourless and quite common. With the addition of metallic oxides, it may become yellow, brown, pink, blue, greenish, orange or sherry. Pale blue stones are found in nature and they have recently, along with colourless topaz, been irradiated with gamma rays to deepen their colour and compete with expensive aquamarine. These stones become an affordable substitute, and the induced colour is stable.

Natural pink topaz is rare and much on the market is induced by heating yellow or sherry crystals. It is also stable.

Hardness: 8. Very hard, but durability is a problem as it has perfect basal cleavage. It could split with a sharp blow. Not recommended for men.

Cuts and shapes: All styles of cutting from mixed to step cuts. We think the more facets the better; and a common champagne colour can sparkle like a million dollars when properly cut.

Sizes: Browns, blues and colourless over 100 cts are impractical but not unusual. In the precious or Imperial colours, over 15 cts is rare in gem quality. Less than one percent of all crystals found are of gem grade and the only commercial deposit is in Auro Preto, Brazil.

If You Are Considering Buying

Topaz is not highly visible, but it is available in the medium, orangey colours of the Imperial variety as well as in the yellows. Retail prices here have been less than in the US and in Brazil. Blue topaz is cut locally and is also readily seen. Most is irradiated and lovely.

Sources for Hong Kong: Brazil, Sri Lanka, Burma and Africa. Topaz is found worldwide except for the Imperial variety.

Uses: Imperial topaz goes well with pumpkin, melon, salmon, peach or apricot coloured clothing. It looks best in white gold settings with diamonds. Definitely for a dinner ring and not for everyday use.

Colourless topaz may be cut and worn as a poor man's diamond. The value is primarily in its cutting costs. It makes an excellent substitute for aquamarine but stands well enough on its own right as a beautiful gem with its own particular characteristics and merits. There is no reason not to own both.

Fair price: Blue — $65 to $150 a carat; Imperials — $600 to $2,500 a carat.

Look for: Freedom from flaws, especially cleavages that could open up with wear or repairs. Look also for your favourite colour and well-proportioned gems exhibiting a velvety body texture with a high lustre. Topaz is heavier than aqua and has a slippery feel to it which becomes apparent after some experience.

Under magnification, large two-phase liquid and gas inclusions may be visible.

Warning

In antiquity all yellow stones were called topaz, and this practice continues today with much quartz sold as "smoky topaz" or "golden topaz". The words "precious" or "Imperial" should precede the golden to sherry qualities of topaz as in "golden Imperial topaz".

The irradiation, however, of yellow precious topaz has caused much alarm in the trade over the past three years. The fantastic orangy-red *is not* stable and fades rapidly (a few hours) when exposed to sunlight. The intense colour is too good to be true, and a knowledgeable buyer's suspicions are immediately aroused. Always heed your instincts concerning gems. (See also *Doctoring of Gems, page 41.*)

Special Care and Feeding

Do not use ultrasonic cleaner. Wash with mild soapy water.

TOURMALINE

Tourmaline is a family or group of interrelated minerals all sharing a common crystal structure and similar chemical composition. It is an infant in the gem world, having been discovered and classified in the late 18th century. The name comes from the Sinhalese word "turamali", meaning "mixed precious stones". As a newcomer it is lacking in folklore, but makes up for it in sheer beauty.

The Chinese have long been fond of tourmaline, and a certain class of Mandarins wore them as buttons. The Imperial Palace in Peking shows many old pieces of green and pink material.

Opaque to transparent depending on the degree of flawlessness.

Colour: The colour range of tourmaline is unsurpassed, and it is a favourite among collectors for its rainbow of colours with all the shades and tones in between. There often exists more than one colour per crystal, and these are called bi- or particoloured.

Another variation displays a core of red with a dark green rind. When this crystal is sliced (much like cutting a slice of salami) these slices are referred to as "watermelon" tourmalines.

The combinations of colours are endless. Solid reds, greens and blues are the most valuable. In general the lighter the colour before becoming washed out, the more desirable.

(a) **Reds:** "Rubellite" ranges from dark red to a medium cherry red. The light reds are categorised as pink tourmaline much as a light ruby is categorised as pink sapphire. Fine reds are scarce. Pinks are most often seen especially in old Chinese jewellery.

(b) **Greens:** The finest green is coloured by chrome and is called chrome tourmaline. It looks like emerald and is rare. Average greens tend towards yellow or blue and blend with the green. An olive tone is common and inexpensive. Local wholesalers may have some fine greens from Africa and Afghanistan.

(c) **Blues:** "Indicolite" is the blue variety, and in its purest hues rivals sapphire. Not often seen in Hong Kong.

(d) **Colourless:** This is the rarest of all and is known to gemmologists as "achroite". It is mainly a collectors' gem.

(e) **Purple** or **violet** is also called "Siberite" as it was once found in Siberia, but it may also be found in other localities.

(f) **Cat's eye tourmaline** is rare and will most often be a bluish green. Fine reds, greens and blues are the most highly prized colours in translucent qualities. Size, colour and sharpness of the eye are important in its evaluation.

Hardness: 7 to 7½ with no cleavage. It is a tough gemstone, very nice for men's jewellery.

Cuts and shapes: Any shape possible, but the most practical is the step cut rectangle which conforms to its hexagonal crystal structure. Large rounds would be the rarest and most beautiful. Pears, ovals and cushions are also attractive with their many facets, producing much life.

Sizes: The normal range for gem quality is one to ten carats, with anything over ten considered collectors' or investment size. Imperfect stones may exceed these limits as crystals are often large.

If You Are Considering Buying

Faceted dark green to olive and soft pinks may be found here. Pendants and art objects are also available. Antique Chinese jewellery using tourmaline cabochons or carvings are expensive.

Sources for Hong Kong: Brazil, Sri Lanka, Afghanistan-Pakistan, Africa.

Ideal for: All types of jewellery. Although we have never seen a man wear tourmaline jewellery it was certainly good enough for the lofty Mandarins, who wore them as symbols of rank.

Look for: Good polish and freedom from inclusions. Be aware of any nicks on the surface.

Inclusions: Generally have thin threadlike cavities running parallel to the length of the crystal. Many tourmalines are free from inclusions, but not the intense reds and blues and the bi- and tri-colours. The lighter in colour the stone, the cleaner it is. Fine clean gems are becoming expensive.

Special Care and Feeding

More frequent cleaning is required, with mild detergent, because tourmaline's electrical properties attract dust.

Warning

Care must be taken in repair work as tourmaline may be damaged by heat.

Because tourmaline is not heavily traded locally, there are few impostors. However, in Brazil glass and synthetic spinel have often passed as natural tourmaline. A simple test with the refractometer or polariscope will generally unveil the impostors.

TURQUOISE

This is one of the oldest recorded gems. It was found by archaeologists in the ancient cultures of Egypt, Tibet and Persia where it was highly prized for its supreme blue colour. In America it is worked by many Southwestern Indians.

Turquoise is *opaque* and found close to the surface of the earth as pebbles or in nodules in arid areas of the world. It is rarely crystallised. The supply in nature is dwindling.

Colours range from baby blue to dark sky blue into greens of low intensity, and may be with or without black matrix lines. With matrix it is aptly called "spiderweb", while the most valuable purest blue variety is called "Persian".

Hardness: Just under 6 and somewhat porous. The more dense, the higher the polish.

Cuts and shapes vary with locality. The North American

Indians prefer to work with irregular or baroque shapes or in small flat or raised pieces for fine inlay work. In other parts of the world most standard shapes and sizes are employed. Beads are either round or irregular-shaped polished nuggets that can be very expensive.

Ideal for all types of jewellery. It looks equally well in silver or gold and can be dressed up or down with or without diamonds. The Persian grade is most often seen in fine jewellery, that with matrix or of greenish colour usually set in silver. It is often combined with coral in Tibetan-type pieces.

If You Are Considering Buying

Small carvings of fine workmanship from China are seen locally using both US and Chinese material. Large nugget snuff bottles may be spotted as well. Persian quality is set in fine jewellery. Turquoise looks well on all skin tones and is especially enjoyed by eastern women. The lighter shades complement fair complexions.

When unset, the stones sell by the piece at Chinese Arts and Crafts and are especially good buys. Most pieces sell by the carat. Hong Kong offers the opportunity to buy fine Persian quality at a reasonable price.

Look for evenness of colour and a pleasing shape. Avoid too heavily matrixed pieces as these are the more likely to break, the matrix being a weak point.

Warning

Much of the turquoise on the market today is treated in a variety of ways to stabilise it or enhance its colour. Wax, oil and plastics are used and should be disclosed to the buyer. This is especially important on goods marked as natural. Get it in writing as to what type or treatment it has had and how long the colour will last. Lots of luck!

Synthetic turquoise is produced by Gilson. It rivals the finest Persian variety but sells for as much as 25 percent less. There is a fair amount on the market in Hong Kong.

MORE ON BUYING

Before You Buy Jewellery

Examine all jewellery as carefully as you would a second-hand car.

Things to Consider

1. **The finish** should be smooth and shiny without noticeable blotches or cracks, especially at the soldering points. Are there rough edges inside or out, especially along channel-set stones? If so, then these need to be smoothed.

2. **Rub prongs over silk** or nylon stockings to see if they catch. If so, the prongs need tightening or smoothing.

3. **Clasps** should be tightly sprung and opened only with some pressure; otherwise they may open accidentally and your jewellery disappear.

4. Good jewellery should have **safety chains** or locks on all clasps.

5. **All prongs should fit snugly** over the stones, and all stones should be fast in their mountings. Prongs or bezels should be repaired if you are able to rotate the stones with your fingernail or hear loose stones jingle when you shake it near your ear (assuming your hearing is good).

6. **All gold should be stamped** with the manufacturer's hallmark and international fineness, e.g. 750 or 18K, 585 or 14K.

7. In most cases **the setting should enhance** the major gem and draw attention to it. In some cases designer pieces of basically precious metals become sculptures and works of art often without gems or with very small ones. Here, the metal is the principal attraction.

8. Jewellery is affected by **fashion** like everything else. Bezel settings are currently "in", often using cabochons and multi-coloured gold settings. Diamonds, rubies, sapphires and

emeralds are fashionable. These are often seen in one piece of jewellery or with one large stone surrounded by dozens of tiny diamonds. The person for whom you are buying jewellery may be fashion conscious and may appreciate something in the latest style. On the other hand, fashions change. When in doubt, consider the ageless, understated classic look.

9. **Matching clothes.** We would like to stress the possibility that the recipient of your jewellery purchase may say "But I have nothing to wear it with", or "I have no clothes that will look good with this".

It is considered tasteful to wear very fancy jewellery with simply-styled, one-colour or subdued coloured clothes. Pearls, diamonds or gold chains look good with almost everything. But coloured gems have to match something. Like the setting, clothes should enhance the stones, especially now that personal "colour analysis" is also fashionable.

Rubies go well if the colours are compatible with a red dress or a multi-coloured dress that has a similar red as a minor colour in the pattern. A light blue aquamarine would look great on a fair-skinned person, preferably blue-eyed, in a dark, blue or white dress.

Aim for contrasts: dark green garnets with a light green dress, for example.

10. **Matching gem and people colours:** A violet blue tanzanite would match Elizabeth Taylor's eyes, a blue-green tourmaline Paul Newman's. Yellow gems look good on blondes or brunettes.

Red gems may not be attractive if the hair is red. A dark green stone complements a ruddy complexion. Amethysts and blue sapphires go nicely with grey hair and do well set in yellow or white gold. See Gem Colour Chart and *Settings and Metals*.

11. **Setting:** See section on *Settings*.

12. **Proportions:** Small, dainty jewellery for small people; heavier-looking jewellery for larger people. Small chains for small stones; heavy, stronger chains for larger stones. Don't

overwhelm a small stone with a fancy, gold and diamond mounting unless it is a very rare gem that demands this attention, such as alexandrite or demantoid garnet.

Earrings. Small ovals and rectangles add little fullness to the face and at times add length. Large rounds or ovals increase fullness in the face. Long danglies are for tall, slim women as they add fullness to the face.

Rings. A large oval ring, marquise or emerald cut is best on long fingers. A small oval or round ring draws attention to long fingers, giving an unattractive lost look. A ring worn on the little finger reduces the overall length of the hand.

Bracelets. One thin bracelet for short, plump arms. More than one bracelet for long, slender arms.

13. **Protection:** A ring of melee diamonds or CZs around an emerald or other fragile stones will help cushion any blows.

14. **Beads and pearls:** Check the drill holes — are there cracks at the openings? Are they oversized? Are they evenly drilled? Place the beads on a flat surface and roll them. If they wobble, they are not even. Two or more uneven strands can be twisted successfully without notice but avoid them if buying only one.

(a) *Sizes.* Shorter strands can have beads of uniform or graduated sizes. If graduated, the smaller beads should be near the clasp and at the back of the neck. Longer strands over 20 inches look best with uniform or slightly graduated bead sizes.

(b) *Knots.* There should be knots in between each bead or at least between the first three or four next to the clasp. In case of breakage, this will minimise loss. It will also keep beads from rubbing up against each other.

(c) *Uniformity* of colour, lustre (pearls only), polish, shape and pattern.

(d) *Strand lengths.* (More for beads than pearls.)

CHOKER: Uniform beads fitting like a dog collar, now in style thanks to Princess Di. Also fashionable are several strands of tiny, freshwater pearls, corals, lapis, amethysts etc.

twisted together. Usually 15″.

A choker broadens and adds fullness to the face. A multi-strand choker will accentuate a long neck.

PRINCESS: 20″-21″. Too long for open-necked blouses but great for sundresses or strapless gowns.

MATINEE: 24″-26″. Be aware that this length and longer can get caught on typewriters or knock over cocktail glasses.

OPERA: 28″-30″. At this length, you might hit amorous midgets in the eye.

BIB: More than three strands of different lengths, the longest 18″. May appear too heavy on small women.

ROPE: 30″-60″, sometimes looped into a big knot but such will damage delicate gems. This length may also be too heavy for small people.

15. **Clasps for pearls:** Good pearls should have proper clasps. Clasps should work easily and close firmly. You should be able to operate them without help. They should be appropriate for the size of the pearls — not too fragile or heavy. A safety catch should be present. Clasps should be attached well to the pearls. Some fancy clasps can be easily detached from the beads and worn as brooches or pendants.

16. **Accents:** Melee diamonds (or CZs) around most dark stones will enhance and bring out the colour of the stone.

17. **Bead holders,** or pearl shorteners, can make beads much more versatile. They can hold beads around the neck like a choker or draw them fetchingly up to one shoulder or tight against the throat.

Warning

Before you hand in your beads to be shortened, knotted or restrung, always count them and have this noted on a receipt. When you get them back, count them again. A jeweller might accidentally leave some behind on the work table.

See also *Buying Techniques, page 21,* for detailed receipts, choosing stones, haggling, introductions, return back policy, sales talk, appraisals and payments.

Made to Order Jewellery

Whether you have three days in Hong Kong or live here, having jewellery made is a worthwhile experience. Your participation with the jeweller-designer makes the delivered ring, pendant or bracelet that much more meaningful and rewarding, to say nothing of the thrill of being able to say that *you* designed it while in Hong Kong!

When choosing a jeweller, examine the jewellery in the shop and try to judge if this store is capable of doing what you want. Most jewellers will not admit that your idea is difficult for them or unviable.

When haggling over price, be aware that a jeweller may attempt to cut corners if you bargain him down *too* much. You get what you pay for.

Get down on paper:

1. **The estimated cost of gold, workmanship and all gems.** This is not normally done here, but there is no reason it can't be. The jeweller must figure out his cost by adding all these parts, along with profit, to give you a final price. The gold estimate may vary and actually be less when the piece is weighed. You may end up with a smaller bill. The other factors are constants, needing no adjustments.

2. **Delivery date,** morning or afternoon. This is especially important if you have to catch a boat or plane. We suggest giving a departure date a day earlier than you are actually leaving to allow for any minor adjustments. Unlike the Brazilians, who are always behind schedule, the Chinese have an excellent record for specified delivery dates, but adjustments are to be expected as you see your creation in three-dimensional form for the first time.

A simple ring could be made in 24 hours while a more complicated piece could take up to a week.

For those of you who live here and say "no rush", be prepared to wait past your expected time as your work will be replaced by "rush" jobs. You must be definite, give a date, and say that you must have it for a special occasion on that date. A phone call a day or two ahead to "check" is worthwhile.

3. **Liability.** Who will be responsible if your stone is damaged or lost during setting? Many jewellers have no liability. Be sure you understand these possibilities and discuss them beforehand.

4. **Refund policy.** Are you obligated, through your deposit (often half of the estimated cost) to take what is made? Will there be a remake without additional charges if you are not thrilled? What if the job is not delivered on time? Will your deposit be refunded?

5. **The design.** This is very important. What you envision may not be what the jeweller interprets. It is best to have a photo or drawing of the piece you want and have the jeweller go over all the parts with you. He will know what is not technically feasible. Make sure you agree on dimensions and the colour of the gold. The local yellow gold is much brighter than most Europeans are used to.

See also *Before You Buy Jewellery, page 109.*

Local Jewellery Designers

Hong Kong has a number of world class jewellery designers. Most of the top prizes for the DIA's Southeast Asia competition have gone to Hong Kong-based designers. See *Diamond.*

Kai-yin Lo sells her designs in prestigious Neiman-Marcus, Bloomingdales, Harrods etc. She has a devoted local following, although our friends who have witnessed her rise to fame can no longer afford her more exclusive pieces. She puts together a unique combination of beads, pearls, antique silver, ivory and jade in a masterful and creative way.

Vickie T'homi of Jade Creations is also recommended for her competitively-priced custom jade pieces and other gems.

Probably some of the best "deals" here are the original

designs talented artists will create for you, often while and work with them. If you go ahead and have the made up, there will be no charge for their efforts.

Although most stores will come up with designs for you in time, there are a number of shops that have designers on the premises. We suggest Jeannie at Sunny Tsui and Maggie at Maggie's Jewellery. If you want to take the design elsewhere to be made up, a charge of $10 to $100 is made.

Compare this with the average price of US$100 you would have to pay for such work in the US and see how many more diamonds you can add to the setting with this saving.

Foreign Imports

True to its international reputation, Hong Kong has a large choice of imported European designer jewellery for the status-conscious Chinese buyer as well as the visitor. After all, if one wears Gucci shoes, carries a Comtesse bag and wears Celine dresses, how can one possibly wear Hong Kong jewellery?

Prices are frequently the same as in the country of origin. Buying here might save you a trip to France and Italy.

See addresses in the *Appendix*.

Antique Jewellery

European

European antique jewellery is not very popular here. Other established markets in the US and Europe dominate the picture, and all attempts to entice the local Chinese have met with minimal success. It seems that to be a true antique, about 100 years are required. This puts us into the Victorian period, which includes mourning jewellery. For the Chinese, anything to do with death is not popular, to say nothing of the rather depressing, sombre colours and designs. Intrinsic value is not related to either.

Some manufacturers here do make reproductions of "period jewellery". This is done not to fool the public, but to fill a market demand. Should you wish to copy an antique from a photo of a museum piece or anything else, you are in the right place. See our section on *Made to Order Jewellery, page 113.*

The best-known stores who know and understand European antiques are: Lane Crawford, Shui Hing, John Allan and The Showroom.

Chinese

You will have much more success finding antique Chinese jewellery. Combination curio-antique shops and the Chinese products stores have trays full of interesting old pieces, some from as far away as Manchuria and Tibet. They are all basically silver with some gold overlay and the gems usually found are coral, turquoise, agate, jade, amber etc. Enamel and the iridescent blue feathers of the kingfisher bird are also seen quite a bit in this jewellery. Some of these kingfisher pieces are done on a form of cardboard. They are mostly hairpins and brooches and it is amazing to see how well preserved many remain despite the delicacy of the feathers.

Many styles of rings exist: rings with frogs, birds and calligraphy designs as well as puzzle rings in four, five or six pieces. They make interesting collections and conversation pieces. Try Charlotte Horstman in Ocean Terminal for a fine collection and knowledgeable sales help.

Carvings

Before you become accustomed to the many carvings that will greet you at every corner, take time to look at them. If this is your first stop in Asia and you think you will want to buy the "big piece" at your last stop, give it some more thought. Our experience is that **this is the place to buy.**

Other Asian cities will have carvings, but more come from Hong Kong or China. Chinese merchants often run the jewellery and curio businesses in other countries with family ties between sources here and outlets there. We have found higher prices in Thailand and even Singapore. China-made goods are generally cheaper here than anywhere else, even China!

The largest selections are at stores specialising in products from China. See *Appendix*. There is a wide range of quality. Most styles are oriental, but more "Western" types are appearing, especially among those made in Hong Kong. It seems that the consumer is getting bored with the classic fairies, goddesses and Buddhas.

The assortment of carving materials is excellent: rock crystal, multicolour fluorite (called green quartz even when it's purple!), rhodochrosite, leopard skin agate, opal, amber, tourmaline, beryl, topaz, jade, ivory, coral, malachite etc.

The finest carvings have traditionally come from Beijing and Shanghai. Fine examples may be readily seen at the Chinese Arts and Crafts stores and many notable curio shops. Those advertising in *Arts of Asia* magazine deserve special attention in this respect.

Some Hong Kong carvers are in a rush to produce, and their work often lacks the quality of detail that makes a fine rather than average piece.

Some of the nicest work here comes from the Chu jade factory and showroom, which you can visit. There you will find tourmaline, agate, jade, to name a few. Pride of workmanship reigns supreme, and you may find a lasting treasure there.

Many factors are involved in evaluating and pricing carvings. Some of them are: type and quality of rough material, time and labour, source of carving, the overall quality of carving, which includes execution of the design by incorporating the various natural colours of the stone, the popularity of the subject and what it represents.

Inspecting

First study the carvings available. Are the proportions good from all points of view? Do they look like what they are supposed to represent? Is there a great deal of detail — texture lines in the clothing and leaves, wrinkles in faces and hands? Are the faces pleasing enough for long-lasting enjoyment or will you tire of them? Are the style or colours compatible with your personality and the personality of your furnishings? Look at the quality of the stone — the polish and balance. Be aware of any chips, scratches or broken parts. Look for glued portions cleverly disguised to make the carving appear as if carved from one entire piece of rough.

The choice of which piece to buy may be difficult. Remember to buy the very best you can afford. Sometimes the best carvings are done on the most humble of gem material, but more often the most valuable material is given to the master carvers.

For the most part, the materials you see here are accurately labelled, especially in the Chinese products stores. The stones seen misrepresented in carvings are:

1. "Colourless rock crystal," actually glass.
2. "Green quartz" or "amethyst", actually green or purple fluorite.
3. "Jade" or "new jade", actually bowenite or serpentine.
4. "Ivory," actually cellulite plastic with or without bone meal added.
5. "Fish bone," actually plastic with bone meal.
6. "Red root amber," actually red plastic.
7. "Aventurine," actually goldstone — aventurine glass.

The above list was compiled over two years of looking and it is offered as a caution.

See *Buying Techniques* and *Customs Regulations*.

Settings and Metals

With the marriage of gems and precious metals come jewels to adorn men and women and enhance their masculinity or femininity; to create allure, and bring prestige and status to all.

The precious metals are platinum, gold and silver. Non-precious metals, less resistant to corrosion, are called base metals, and may be copper, iron or nickel. All may be used for jewellery.

METALS

Platinum is the rarest and most valuable of the precious metals. It is also the hardest (4-4½) and longest lasting. Its inherent chemical stability accounts for its beautiful enduring lustre. To date, the earth has yielded a mere 1,700 tons of this white metal compared to 100,000 tons of gold.

Actually, platinum is composed of six elements: platinum, iridium, osmium, palladium, rhodium and ruthenium. Pure platinum is marked Pt. 1,000. Any purity lower than this is a combination of the six above metals and should be marked accordingly:

95% — Pt. 950
90% — Pt. 900
85% — Pt. 850

The standard purity for platinum now on the market is Pt. 900. Should the purity go below 90 percent, all of the other elements must be listed on the piece according to their content, such as "Plat. 700, Pall. 200, Irid. 100" — all adding up to 1,000 or 100 percent.

Platinum is more difficult to work than gold because of its extreme hardness. It will hold gems better and cost more in settings than gold. It is traded locally along with pure gold in the form of jewellery and in tael weights. Daily quotes are posted in gold shops and, although more valuable than gold worldwide, it will at times sell for less, a phenomenon of supply and demand. The Chinese historically prefer gold.

Gold — "Everlasting Treasure" — knows no equal. Its history fills volumes and its study never ceases to amaze.

1. All the gold so far found on earth is said to be able to make a 54 ft cube.

2. One ounce may be drawn out into a wire 50 miles long.

3. One ounce may be rolled so that it can cover an area of 100 sq. ft.

4. Pure gold (no alloys present) is not affected by time or the elements. Artifacts discovered from 3,200 BC look like new.

Gold in Hong Kong comes in different purities, all measured by carats for the international jewellery market. Carats is spelled "Karats" in the US, and both terms are used here. Gold is weighed, however, in taels for the local bullion market.

GOLD — Weights and Measures

1 troy oz. = 0.831 tael
1 tael = 1.20337 troy oz.
1 gram = 0.03215 troy oz.
1 gram = 0.02672 tael

Multiply the number of taels by 1.20337 **to convert taels to troy ounces.** With the resulting figure you can compare prices here with those elsewhere. The latest gold prices quoted in troy ounces on the London, New York and Hong Kong markets can be found in the *Asian Wall Street Journal* and the *South China Morning Post.*

The Chinese have traditionally invested in **pure gold** in the form of jewellery, ornaments and tael bars. Hong Kong is the largest market in the world for 24K gold. They call it *Chuk Kam*, and no ceremony is complete without its presence. You have only to peer into a crowded restaurant at a wedding party. The bride is usually laden down with fancy necklaces and bracelets. Observe the guests as well. And note how beautiful the yellow metal is with the traditional red wedding gown. No wonder rubies are so popular with the Chinese. Red is the colour of happiness and it goes so well with gold.

Chuk Kam satisfies many needs: status, ornamental and a hedge against inflation. It also provides an instant bank account as it may be sold back any time for the current gold price.

The profit margin for selling Chuk Kam is a mere seven percent, which includes labour and profit. King Fook does run a yearly sale on Chuk Kam with no labour charges. Compare the price of Italian 18K gold chains of similar appearance and see if you don't agree that the price of Chuk Kam is a good investment.

You may also enjoy a change of style if you buy a Chinese chain, bracelet, earrings and small pendants. How about your own Chinese zodiac animal? Why not a solid gold sculptured pig or horse or whatever for that curio cabinet or pendant? See *Chinese Calligraphy in Jewellery* in the *Appendix, page 155.*

Chuk Kam, pure gold, is listed as "99.99" and is marked with the company's special chop and "pure gold" in Chinese. As pure gold, it is very soft and malleable. The solid gold clasp is soft and you must open and close it carefully. Bend one end backwards only far enough to open or close. Never pull it sideways as if breaking a wishbone or you will break it within a short period. The clasps all look like this

and are actually copies of ancient clasp pieces.

If one should break, it can be repaired while you wait in most gold shops. We suggest buying chains that can be put over your head without opening unless you live in a place where you can have the clasp repaired regularly.

No solder is used to make Chuk Kam jewellery. Pieces are joined by "sweating" gold to the point of flowing and then cooling it in the proper positions, a tricky and specialised skill.

Gold coins are also sold here either as collectors' pieces or as bullion, with daily price quotes just like Chuk Kam. They are usually 20-21K.

Chuk Kam is sold in many shops, large and small. The ones we are most familiar with are King Fook, Chow Tai Fook, Manning, Deak Perera, Chow Sang Sang and Henry's. For those of you more interested in traditional **karat gold,** Hong Kong sells mostly 14K and 18K made locally or imported from the US and Italy. At times you may see 9K and 12K stamped on pieces. These two were used for less expensive jewellery and are not seen a great deal today. Also in the past some pieces were marked 14K that were only 9K. This occurred before the current attempt to control gold fineness.

Hong Kong Tourist Association member shops must mark their gold for fineness with an identifying hallmark.

Pure gold is only 2½ on the hardness scale. Because of its softness and malleability, other metals have to be added to strengthen it. These metals are called alloys. The amount of alloy determines the karat or fineness. Finenesses of 9K and 12K are not recommended because the lower karat gold is less resistant to corrosion and more brittle. Gold is not marked for

GOLD PURITY

US	Europe	
24K	.999	99.99% to 99.6% pure gold and known locally as Chuk Kam
22K	.916	22 parts gold to two parts other metals — 91.6%
18K	.750	18 parts gold to six parts other metals — 75% pure
14K	.585	14 parts gold and ten parts other metals — 58.5% pure
10K	.416	10 parts gold and 14 parts other metals — 41.6% pure

karat fineness if below 10K in the US or 9K in Britain.

"Solid gold" means that the gold content is found throughout the metal (including alloy) and not just on the surface.

A good-looking "gold" ring stamped "925" should also have "sterling" written on it because it is made of silver and most likely gold plated. This plating will wear off in time depending on the thickness of the gold plate. Electroplating is measured in microns. Top gold-plated items have 10-25 microns whereas most jewellery pieces have only two to three. Gold wash or flash jewellery has even less, with only 0.18 microns or 7 millionths of an inch of gold accumulation. This type of jewellery is usually costume type and inexpensive.

It is difficult to test accurately for gold fineness. Many jewellers will test gold by rubbing the object on a "touchstone" and applying acid. How the two interact indicate the karat rating. A more complicated and often destructive test is used if necessary for complete accuracy.

The type of metal alloy incorporated determines the colour of the gold. Let your preference be known when you custom order.

Gold Alloys Used for Colours	
Pink	— copper
Yellow	— copper and silver
Green	— cadmium and silver
	— silver
	— copper and zinc
Blue	— iron
White	— copper, zinc and nickel, palladium, nickel
Purple	— aluminium, zinc
Copper and silver	— natural copper and silver.

Note: The higher the gold content, combined with alloying

metal, the more yellow the gold. The proportions of gold used control karat content.

Silver. Although silver will tarnish and corrode, it is nevertheless a precious metal and was valued even in 4000 BC.

Pure silver is 99.99 percent. It is too soft to be worked without an alloy. Copper is usually used but in smaller amounts than alloying gold. Sterling silver is 92.5 percent pure silver and 7.5 percent copper, and standard international markings are "sterling", "925", or "92.5 fine". Coin silver is sometimes found in jewellery and is 90 percent pure.

Silver is only 2½ to 3 on the hardness scale and is easily scratched. Many manufacturers will plate silver with rhodium to give it a bright tarnish-free finish. Uncoated silver, if worn regularly, resists tarnishing. Of course, common sense dictates that you take off any silver when swimming in the sea because salt attacks silver and pits and tarnishes it.

Many beautiful and inexpensive decorative stones may be put into silver mountings and electroplated with gold. The labour will be approximately the same but the savings in using the silver will be considerable. When the gold plating wears thin, it may be replated at a small cost. Cubic zirconia (the diamond simulants) look super in silver mountings with a rhodium bath and gold plate.

Suggested store: Men's Jewellery Centre. Full range of handmade silver puzzle rings, identification bracelets, signet rings etc.

SETTINGS

Most settings here are **handmade.** However, for mass production, castings are used. Melted gold is poured into a rubber mould and allowed to harden. The quality of the cast piece depends on the technique and skill of the producer and may be as good or better than a handmade article.

Prices are generally lower for castings due to economy of time and labour.

Setting styles

1. *Open setting using prongs or claws* — Either high or low with four, six or eight prongs used. An open setting shows off the stone best, as light enters from all angles.

2. *Closed or bezel* — No prongs used. The stone is surrounded by metal like a rim, with or without a closed back. This setting minimises the danger of losing stones but reduces brilliance.

3. *Pave* (pronounced pah-vay) — Usually with small diamonds. The studded effect is achieved by gouging tiny strips of gold from a closed mounting and dropping a diamond in each recess and pushing up more gold against the girdle of the diamond to hold it fast. This thereby creates a new spot for the next diamond.

4. *Channel* — Very popular at the moment. Two channels of gold are created that look like railroad tracks with parallel grooves set into the tracks just below the surface. The stones, usually small diamonds, are slipped tightly into the grooves. The effect is clean, especially with square cut stones.

5. *Invisible* — Is relatively new here, and this technique has been mastered by only a few of the most accomplished goldsmiths. It involves setting small, perfectly matched stones without any gold showing, a virtual bed of colour and texture.

Finishes

These may be *polished*, *florentine* or *matte*, all of which are subject to fashion. Currently the polished look is "in". Polished gold will obviously need repolishing as well and should be considered when having your yearly check-up for loose stones and ageing prongs. A florentine, cross-hatched textured surface will wear smooth with time and may be restored.

When ordering a ring: It is important to show the jeweller just what type and what dimensions of *shank* or *band* you prefer. People with short knuckles and chubby fingers may be uncomfortable with wide bands. A thinner one may be more attractive on your hand. It is definitely cheaper, using less gold.

Proportions are important. A 30-carat aquamarine on a band meant for a half-carat diamond would be ridiculous. State your preference to the jeweller and then listen to his suggestions.

Height of stone: Avoid misunderstandings regarding the intended height of a setting off your finger. Deeply cut gems will require a predetermined minimum of height, whereas shallower stones give you more choice. Spell it out and show examples from something in the shop if need be.

A stone set high is more easily broken or caught but, especially with diamonds, the stones look more brilliant. For designers see addresses in *Appendix, Local Designers* and *Diamond* (for diamond design award winners).

Stone and Metal Combinations

The colour of gold in combination with certain coloured stones may surprise you. For example, keep an open mind when the jeweller suggests that the aquamarine you have selected would look better in a platinum or white gold mounting. Just because you have only yellow gold jewellery does not mean that your aqua will look its best in yellow gold. In fact, most aquas are set in white metals because yellow combines with the blue to produce a greenish cast to the stone, replacing what the heat treatment took away. See *Aquamarine*.

The ultimate compromise if you insist on yellow gold for setting a sky blue aqua is a white metal prong or bezel setting, with a yellow gold shank or band. Now you have satisfied the need to remain with your yellow gold but you have not sacrificed the beauty of the stone. This type of combining two metals is a bit more costly and time-consuming for the jeweller, but well worth the investment in beauty and for achieving a professional look.

Be aware of the poor practice of coating yellow gold with a rhodium bath to turn it white. The jeweller may have bought fifty yellow gold rings at a bargain but needed ten white golds for his stock. He rhodium-plated these to solve his problem. In time they will revert back to yellow and you will need to repeat the process.

Diamonds, if white and not yellowish, look best set in white prongs. Again, the rest of the setting may be done in yellow gold. But white diamonds will look their best reflecting off the white metal. Should you choose slightly yellowish diamonds, they will actually look *whiter* if set in yellow gold. Sounds confusing, but take a look and see for yourself.

As a general rule, the cool gem colours (blues, greens, purples) look best in white metal and the warm colours (red, orange and yellow) look best in yellow gold.

Shopping for Other People

This is one of the most thankless tasks, so avoid it if possible. If you cannot, you might be successful if the person who wants you to "pick up" a jade ring pays in advance and gives you either a lot of latitude ("I'll be happy with *any* green jade ring that you like and fits your little finger") or very specific instructions. Remember, a lot of time can be frittered away on what may seem initially a simple request.

The specific instructions should be written down and safeguarded. The best possible help would be a picture of the item he has in mind. You need to know the size, karat and colour of gold, type of setting and how much he wants to spend. It is better to have a wide range. For example, if you can't get 14K white gold, how about yellow gold? You don't want to get involved with long distance phone calls over a $100 cost differential.

It is better to overestimate on a ring size, if you don't know the correct one. It can easily be made smaller.

Gemmologists as Guides

With the high interest in gems and jewellery in Hong Kong and the availability of gem study through the British Diploma

Course and the Gemological Institute of America, there are a number of qualified resident gemmologists. These are Fellows of the Gemmological Association of Great Britain and certified graduate gemmologists.

Many of these knowledgeable persons are not employed full time, and they are well qualified, with a keen knowledge of the local market. They can be contacted to help you try to save time and money.

Full and half-day shopping "sprees" can be arranged on a flat rate for up to four persons per guide. This service is not limited to jewellery, for the guides know other dimensions of the Hong Kong market as well. Some foreign languages are spoken by these gemmologists, who have lived in many parts of the world and are of different nationalities.

Interested parties can contact the author, Joan Ahrens, at 5-930478, for more details.

Gems and Jewellery Recommended for Men

Men enjoy a newly-regained freedom and acceptance of their adorning themselves with jewellery. It has been many centuries since men have worn more than one ring, owned two or more watches, dangled gold chains around their necks and wrists and, for the very avant-garde, pierced an ear or nostril!

What a wonderful time women can have by exchanging accepted roles and buying jewellery for their husbands! Why not surprise them? Now is the time to express your appreciation for this trip to Hong Kong by bringing back one of those little "goodies" that he always brings you.

Our advice is to select chains that you can both share if Mr Macho Man feels they are too feminine regardless of style. If you think he would appreciate a gem, consider:

Lapis lazuli
Tiger's eye
Tourmaline cat's eye

Jade in all colours (what is his favourite colour?)
Black star sapphire
Cat's eye chrysoberyl
Star ruby and star sapphire
Diamond
Blue sapphire.

Possible types of jewellery: Rings, tie tacks or tie bars, cufflinks (for both of you), chains and bracelets. Other precious metal accessories: Money clips (engraved or with a stone), lighter, cigarette holder or a gem-faced watch.

Care and Protection of Jewellery

1. Nothing distresses jewellery lovers and gemmologists more than to see stones in beautiful settings dirtied by the accumulation of hand creams, cookie dough, soap film and garden dirt.

It is a shame to have a bag of jewellery arrive for appraisal with the pieces all jumbled up together and dumped on our desks. We can all but imagine the cries as the diamonds, the hardest of the gems, scratch into the softer amethysts, which in turn tumble into the even more fragile opals — to say nothing of what is happening to the beautiful metals that will need repolishing to bring back their gorgeous lustre.

Each piece should be separated, stored in padded boxes or silk bags, and removed from the hand when gardening, doing dishes, kneading dough etc.

Jewellery stores give silk bags with each sale. Use them. You can also buy extras for gifts. Just make sure they have zippers so you won't lose tiny items. Most travellers prefer the bag for travelling convenience, but a box offers added protection, especially for the more delicate gems.

2. Men and women tend to treat their jewellery differently. Have you noticed that we recommend some stones for women but not for men? This is because men tend to wear their

jewellery all the time. Men who work with their hands or who play sports should be aware that basketball players have had their fingers separated when their rings were caught on hoops. Some construction workers foolish enough to work while wearing rings or bracelets have had ghastly accidents, and Texas and Oklahoma pawnshops are filled with the smashed diamond rings of oil rig crews.

Women tend to misplace jewellery, especially rings, when they remove them for washing hands or doing the odd job. They often put on earrings over the bathroom sink where they may slip and disappear down the drain. Plug the drain!

3. During **cold weather,** rings will loosen because fingers contract. This combined with soap can cause a ring to come off your finger and escape down the drain before you realise it.

4. Stones can **become loose** due to careless workmanship or because of dirt. Shake your jewellery and listen for a rattle or use your fingernail to see if the stones are loose. If so, take them to a jeweller.

Dirty jewellery that has been ignored for years may have undetected loose stones. Dirt becomes wedged between the stone and the prongs and pushes them apart. When the dirt is eliminated, the stone may even fall out.

5. Small model ultrasonic jewellery cleaners are now available and their use is *not* recommended *except* by professionals. The same goes for steam. As a rule of thumb, stones over $7\frac{1}{2}$ on the hardness scale may be cleaned with ammonia or jewellery cleaner. Clean stones under $7\frac{1}{2}$ only with mild soap and warm water.

6. **Never hang up beads** to dry but lay them flat on a towel.

7. **Chemicals:** *Household bleach* can discolour settings. *Ammonia* reacts with copper found in some settings. *Chlorine* used in swimming pools has been found to dissolve karat gold over a three-month period of constant immersion. It does nothing, of course, to pure gold.

8. While swimming in the sea, it is best to remove all jewellery, as you may lose it. Many fish, like barracudas, are attracted to anything shiny.

9. Some stones fade in **sunlight** or change colour due to **temperature extremes.**

10. **Ordinary plastic bags** may be harmful to some metals and especially to organic gems like coral, pearls, opal, amber and ivory, which need to "breathe". There are specially prepared plastic bags that jewellers may purchase which are safe.

Repairing, Polishing and Cleaning Jewellery

Prices for renovating jewellery are cheaper in Asia than in most other places in the world. Just to be sure, check with your jeweller at home first. Then get an estimate here.

The advantage of having jewellery done in Hong Kong is the high quality of the workmanship. Jewellers here will also do many things for **free** or for nominal prices, such as restringing beads, tightening prongs, seizing (without solder), polishing and cleaning.

SERVICE	US$ IN THE US	HK$ IN HONG KONG
Pearl stringing	$1 an inch	Free or $30 to $40 a strand
Enlarging ring size		
thin	$10	$50 to $150
medium	$15	
wide	$20	
Decreasing ring size		
thin	$10 to $15	$50 to $75
medium		
wide		
Solder break in thin chain	$8	Free to $30

Custom design drawing	$75 to $150	Free if work is ordered or $15 to $150
Rebuild one prong		
over diamond	$10 then $8 each additional	$10 to $25
over coloured stone	$20 then $10 each additional	
Soldering charm to bracelet	$8 then $5 each additional	
Bale for pendant	$15 to $45	$60 to $120
Repolish cabochon	$5 to $10	$10 to $15
Repolish table of coloured stone	$30 an hour	$20 to $45
Gold plate a ring	$15 to $40	$30 to $200
Rhodium plate ring	$25	$10 to $20

White gold is slightly higher priced than yellow gold because of the more expensive alloys. Sometimes the cost difference is absorbed by the jeweller, and other times you are charged more. In Hong Kong, add approximately 15 percent for white gold and 25 percent for 18K to the above 14K prices. Some shops here charge a flat $100 to $200 increase depending on the weight.

In Hong Kong many services are provided without undue profits, while in the US service is an important source of income.

These prices which we have collected are indicators only and stores will have individual policies and prices.

Replacing a Gem

Locating a stone for an existing setting sounds easy. Try it before reading this and see how successful you are. Hopefully, this will save you aggravation and you will achieve your goal.

Suppose your wife lost a five-carat tourmaline and wants

you to bring her a new one from Hong Kong. You know it was round and pink. That should be easy enough. One five-carat round pink tourmaline coming up!

You find a shop here that sells loose stones and has a parcel of round pink tourmalines. You are in luck and it couldn't have been easier. You select the prettiest five-carat stone and off you go.

Back home, with much pride, you present the stone to your wife, who then proceeds to drop it into the barren setting. And drop it she does, right through to the floor.

What could have gone wrong?

The stone was too small in size (mm.) though of proper weight.

For best results:

1. Bring the piece of jewellery with you for resetting. Travel with the original sales receipt or any other document stating prior ownership. You will only need to claim the new stone and labour charges for Customs upon your return.

If this is not possible, then:

2. Have the millimetre size of the opening recorded as well as the depth of the mounting. If you buy a stone that is too deep, it will go below the mounting and hit the finger.

3. If you find a stone too small by a fraction of a millimetre, the setting can usually be adjusted to fit. If the stone is too large for the mounting, have the stone recut while here to fit exactly.

If you need to replace one gem variety with another, a lost garnet with an amethyst, for example, be aware that a six-carat garnet is much smaller than a six-carat amethyst due to their difference in specific gravity. Again you need the millimetre measurements to fill that empty setting accurately.

See also *Customs Regulations* in the *Appendix*.

ECONOMICS

Insurance and Appraisals

Insurance

According to insurance company surveys, only 40 percent of all jewellery claims are made against stolen goods. The majority is LOST. Basically there are two types of insurance for jewels, which are briefly:

Homeowners: Which covers personal property including jewellery, but only to a limited extent. Fire, theft, mysterious disappearance, tornadoes etc. may be listed as individual clauses. The greatest number of claims is for "mysterious disappearance". Without this clause in your policy, you have little protection.

Most homeowners have a *deductible clause* as well. You are not reimbursed for the total insured value if you make a claim. Unless your piece is very valuable, it may not be worth insuring. You would be covered for all but the deductible portion.

Inland marine, "floater" or *"all-risk" policies* usually include anything mobile: cameras, jewellery, golf clubs etc. There is no deductible clause and you receive the full insured value of your claim. Rates are fixed based upon overall statistics as to how much the company receives in premiums and pays out in claims.

At one time men were considered higher risks than women for loss due to carelessness and by the nature of their jobs. Some companies still charge more for men and more for high crime rate areas. It is best to compare companies before selecting one.

For expatriates, it is important to check your existing policies for *living abroad*. Some only allow for one year out of the country for coverage and then you are on your own — your policy null and void.

There are many good insurance companies represented in Hong Kong. A few do special work with jewellery and gems. Mollers' Insurance Agents (HK) Ltd and Tai Koo Royal Insurance Co. Ltd have been brought to our attention through trade and personal contacts.

Appraisals

Appraisals at first glance might seem simple and basic. Their purpose is to determine current market value or replacement costs. However, upon further investigation one sees just how complicated these may become. We will attempt to simplify the procedure for you by mentioning the most important areas.

Valuables should be *professionally* appraised: for insurance purposes, estates, inheritance taxes, Customs declarations, selling and trading back for more expensive goods. You may need to know the replacement value at home for a piece bought abroad.

The appraisal should be current for any of the above, as the ring you bought six years ago could easily be worth today three or four times what you paid.

Be aware that there are several types of appraisals:

1. *Retail Replacement Value*, defined as the amount it would cost to buy the same piece today in a jewellery store.

2. *Estate Appraisal* reflects the current day-to-day market value — what the piece would sell for to a willing buyer. This price is often the wholesale price and is always lower than retail replacement value. This is primarily for inheritance taxes — what it could be sold for immediately to clear an estate.

3. *Selling Appraisal* is usually below wholesale. It reflects what a dealer would be willing to pay. This appraisal is usually used for distress sales.

A replacement evaluation might be $1,000, an estate value $700, and a selling appraisal $450. All three are valid for the same item and have their own purposes.

Charges for appraisals are usually a fixed fee or a

percentage of the appraised value, not more than 1½ percent. If given a choice, we prefer the less biased flat fee. Another possibility would be an hourly fee.

The Appraiser

Just because someone puts up a sign stating he can appraise and evaluate jewellery is no sure measure of his experience. A degree holder who has never worked in the trade is no more equipped to sign an appraisal for a rare "coronel murta" aquamarine than is a postman. Nor is a jeweller who has never studied gemmology. Experience combined with technical learning are the key ingredients.

Antique jewellery needs a specialist in that area. How else can intrinsic value be placed on a piece normally valued for the combination of all its parts, with no value levied on rarity and history?

To Choose an Appraiser Check For:

1. Gemmological training from an internationally recognised gemmological institute like the Gemmological Association of Great Britain or the Gemological Institute of America. Hong Kong is fortunate in having many FGAs and GGs from these associations. Many are staff members of prestigious jewellery firms here.

2. Trade experience; buying and selling of gems and jewellery.

3. Lab facilities and up-to-date equipment. These should include microscope, refractometer, polariscope, spectroscope, diamond balance, heavy liquids, thermal conductivity tester, sodium light source, master set of diamonds and ultraviolet light.

4. What trade organisations he belongs to and what trade journals he subscribes to.

5. How fees are charged.

6. How the appraisal is carried out and what his responsibilities and liabilities are to you.

The appraisal itself must be complete and to the point. It must cover all of the following in writing on an official form with the letterhead of the appraiser. For example, a retail replacement appraisal would have:

1. All stones listed by quantity, identification, shape, dimensions in millimetres, weight or computed approximate weight and quality of colour and cutting; e.g. 3 ct oval, 6 mm. × 4.5 mm., fine medium dark Ceylon blue sapphire of fine proportions and good polish.

2. Fineness of gold and type of mounting (handmade or casting); e.g. 14K yellow gold handmade setting.

3. Estimate of retail replacement value.

4. Existing damage to any parts. This should be noted and acknowledged by the owner in writing or on the "take-in" form.

5. List of tests performed and equipment used.

All appraisal forms should be dated, signed by the appraiser with copies for the owner/customer, insurance company (if applicable) and the store records. Do not confuse an appraisal with a certificate of identification where no value is given.

If you are not satisfied with one appraisal, try another company.

Gems and Jewellery as Investments

Five or six years ago we would have recommended gems, if not jewellery, as a good form of investment. Much has happened to change this. The investment diamond, precious metals and coloured stone market crashed in 1981. The world economy came to a near halt with inflation and high interest rates. Those people who were ill-informed as to the liquidity of their holdings found themselves in a very bad way. No one was buying, at least not at the super levels held prior to this.

With big risks come big profits or losses, and the gem investment field is no different. It is a speculative market that requires much research into buying habits the world over and up-to-date knowledge of what gems are being discovered, who is buying on a monthly basis etc. Very few people outside of the trade have any idea how complicated this is.

We do not recommend investment buying for the amateur.

Gems should be bought for two reasons: for transforming them into pieces of jewellery to be worn and loved, or for a collection to be enjoyed, much as stamps, shells or coins are. This hobby is worldwide and growing rapidly with fine collectors' gems always in short supply. Collections do offer a genuine hedge against inflation, because fine gems continue to increase in value; however, it may take time.

Always buy the finest you can afford and upgrade at every opportunity. Even during the height of the investment craze, reputable dealers advised the holding of gems for a three to five year period before attempting to resell for a profit.

When you are thinking of reselling, just remember that whatever price sheets quote as the going price for any gem, **the actual price is always the function of what the market will bear.** Sapphires not selling well in Los Angeles may find an eager market in Paris. But how will you get the parcel there, and who do you know and trust to handle them? Before you know it, you become a gem merchant just to protect your own interest.

Investments as they relate to jewellery are slightly different from loose stones. Jewellery takes more time to catch up with retail prices should you want to sell. Retail prices include labour, mounting and a high profit. At the same time, jewellery depreciates with wear and tear and must be restored. You cannot expect to get even what you paid for it immediately.

In both cases, the only way you will realise your "investment" is to find a private buyer, or wait for the jewellery to appreciate and then try again.

APPENDIX

Customs Regulations

The wise person interested in jewels and gems should check the Customs regulations for his own country and for those countries through which he will be passing. The main concern of Customs officials is for **endangered animals** like elephant and whale.

Since regulations are constantly changing, we urge you to keep current on any items you are carrying or intend to carry in or through these countries. We can only give you a rough idea of what to expect.

For example, it has been forbidden to bring into Hong Kong, **without a prearranged permit,** either of these two endangered species, dead or alive, in part or whole. A Customs officer need only *suspect* that the animal product you have is on the endangered list and he has the authority to seize it. It may later be returned if, in fact, it is proven not to be one of the endangered species. This checking will take precious time.

In addition, these animal parts can be seized **even while in transit.** They cannot be kept in bond at the airport to be taken out later.

Technically, regulations in regard to gem and jewellery items have required the confiscation of parts of non-domestic cats (like tiger's claws), elephant (ivory), marine turtles, rhino (horns) and whales (teeth and bone).

This endangered species list has also applied to other countries who have signed the Convention on Endangered Species to protect these animals from extinction.

The exception to this ruling has been in the area of antiques. For example, certified antiques have been legally imported into the US. Collectables such as rhino horn cups, snuff bottles and carvings have been confiscated unless the owner could prove their antiquity, which has meant "made prior to 1830"! Australian antiques have been "over 100 years old". Canada has said "at least 100 years old".

We must point out that any Customs officer has **the right to dispute any certificate you may present** and we suggest that you be prepared to surrender any of these items upon entry.

African elephant ivory has been permitted into some countries like the US **for personal use** without a certificate of origin, **unless mailed.** In some of these countries this has meant not just non-commercial use but also gifts. Since 95 percent of the elephant ivory sold in Hong Kong is of African origin, this has not been a problem for the tourist buying items for himself.

Be aware, however, that other countries have had more stringent regulations than the US. Germany, for example, has demanded an **export certificate** issued by Hong Kong's Agricultural and Fisheries Department for all ivory, regardless of origin. Without it, there has been the danger of **confiscation** by German Customs officials, even if you are only passing through Germany.

Shopkeepers may charge you their cost price of about $40 to acquire an export certificate for mailing parcels.

The importation of scrimshaw and *netsuke* (small carvings and pendants) made of whale, dolphin or porpoise, teeth or bones is also forbidden by some countries, especially the US.

For some countries, **registering your jewellery** before you leave home is a good idea. This has been to avoid Customs duties on previously-owned jewellery. Americans and some other nationals have been advised to carry either jewellery appraisals, insurance certificates or original receipts of all jewellery in their possession.

Remember **it is up to you to prove prior ownership.** Everything in your possession could be assumed to be new.

It is unwise to burden yourself with too much jewellery while travelling today. The risk of theft is high.

You should also be aware that countries have charged **different rates of duty for different gems and jewellery.** The US, for example, has charged 19.3 percent on costume jewellery, 9.2 percent on fine jewellery and about 2.3 percent on most unset stones. Emeralds have been duty free. Australia has charged nothing on unset stones.

Be aware of the complications of set and unset gems.

For the US, temporarily strung cultured pearls have been taxed at 2.3 percent. If permanently strung with a precious metal clasp, the tax rate has been levied on the more expensive part, the clasp or the pearls. If the chief value is the metal, then it has been 9.2 percent, the same as all precious gold metal jewellery. If the chief value is the pearls, 19.3 percent duty has applied.

Don't attempt to bring in the proposed clasp with the pearls temporarily strung, or they will be judged as strung and the higher rate of duty charged. Better to figure out how much restringing costs at home and how much a clasp would be. Which scheme works out better for you?

Many countries have **duty free** allowances for returning tourists, business people and returning non-residents coming home for vacations. **Each category has different allowances.**

These duty free allowances may have complications. For example, American tourists have been allowed $400 duty free exemptions on goods bought abroad. They have had to pay 10 percent on the next $1,000 worth **even if this has included unset gems normally dutiable at 2.3 percent.** Over the $1,000, each item has been taxed according to its own tax schedule.

Items with the highest rate of duty are usually listed first for the $400 duty free allowance.

Note also that some **carvings** done in Hong Kong have

been admitted either duty free or taxed at a lower rate than carvings made in China. American trade regulations differ. Jade and coral carvings from Hong Kong have been duty free but taxed at 21 percent if carved in China. Not many years ago, nothing was allowed in from China.

Antiques are usually duty free in many countries, but proof is up to the purchaser. Check with Customs in your own country what documents are needed and where these can be obtained. Usually a receipt is sufficient.

Make sure that the **origin of work** is stated on your **sales receipt.** Normally duty free jewellery and stones from Thailand, for example, when bought in Hong Kong, have been taxed as Hong Kong goods by US Customs. The purchase money went to Hong Kong, not Thailand.

Customs duties are imposed, no matter where, **according to the discretion and often the mood of the officer on duty.** On one confrontation you might claim $1,000 and be charged $5 duty in five minutes. On another trip the same officer may take 20 minutes and make you pay $60 for the same thing.

Honesty is always advisable, and in some countries you can negotiate with the Customs officer or appeal against his judgement to his superiors.

For updated regulations and further questions concerning Customs, please consult the appropriate representative from the list below. It is even better to check with Customs in your home country **before you leave,** because representatives here may not know all the current regulations.

Important Telephone Numbers and Addresses
CONSULATES AND COMMISSIONS

Australia: 5-227171
Austria: 5-239716, 5-247398
Belgium: 5-7907321

Britain: 5-230176
Canada: 5-282222
Denmark: 5-256369
France: 5-294351
Germany: 5-298855, 5-284475
Greece: 5-243419
India: 5-272275, 5-284028
Italy: 5-220033
Japan: 5-96363
Korea: 5-437562
Malaysia: 5-270921
Netherlands: 5-227720, 5-227718, 5-227719
New Zealand: 5-255047
Norway: 5-749253
Pakistan: 5-274623
Philippines: 5-7908823
Singapore: 5-247091
Spain: 5-253041
Sri Lanka: 5-8915204
Sweden: 3-9220221
Switzerland: 3-7220333
Thailand: 5-728705
United States: 5-239011, X244

RETAIL STORES

(NOTE: We regret that we cannot guarantee any company or store. The following are only mentioned to help you find what you are looking for.)

CODE

AAA — exclusive in design, selection and workmanship. Variety of stones with generally one or two specialities such as pearls, diamonds or jade.

AA — good selection of merchandise with more of a price range to choose from than AAA. May also specialise in one area.

A — variety of goods; may be smaller, less overhead offering more personalised service.

With any type of ranking system, one always has overlapping areas. Ours is a simple means to help the reader know what to expect in the way of size and pricing structure of the stores listed. These are not indicative of reliability.

A specifically listed item denotes speciality in that area, e.g. pearls, diamonds etc. We suggest you telephone first to ask if they have what you want.

NOTE: "TST" means Tsim Sha Tsui, the area encompassing the Star Ferry, New World Centre and north to Kowloon Park. "C" is for Central, on Hong Kong island within walking distance of the Star Ferry and around the Central MTR station. "Causeway Bay" is on Hong Kong island near the Cross-Harbour Tunnel and between the Lee Gardens, Plaza and Excelsior hotels. "GG" and "FGA" refer to trained, graduate gemmologists.

Stores specialising in products from China. Prices are reasonable and should be used as a measuring stick for anything else you might buy in Hong Kong. Generally very reliable. Prices are fixed but five to ten percent discount "Privilege Cards" are available on request for visitors and residents, usually from the Overseas Chinese Service Department.

The Chinese Arts and Crafts stores and the Chung Kiu Chinese Products Emporium are near the top of the market, with prices to match. They offer a good selection of carvings, jewellery and unset stones: turquoise, agate, coral, lapis, malachite, diamonds, rubies, sapphire, soapstone, jade, ivory, bone, sodalite, etc.

Chinese Arts & Crafts (H.K.) Ltd, G34-35 New World Centre, TST. Tel. 3-697760; Star House (near Star Ferry), TST. Tel. 3-674061; 233-9 Nathan Road, Yaumatei, Kowloon. Tel. 3-670061; Shell House, Queen's Road and Wyndham Street, C. Tel. 5-266758. *Silvercord*, 30 Canton Road, TST.

Chung Kiu Chinese Products Emporium Ltd, 17 Hankow Road, TST. Tel. 3-7233211.

All-purpose department stores sell gems and jewellery. Quality may be as good as the above and prices and selection may be less.

China Products Co. (H.K.) Ltd, Lok Sing Centre, Yee Wo Street, Causeway Bay (same street as Plaza Hotel, by Victoria Park). Tel. 5-7908321. This store is larger than the other one in Causeway Bay at Percival Street and Hennessy Road.

Chinese Merchandise Emporium Ltd, 92-104 Queen's Road C., (across from the Central Market). Tel. 5-241051.

Yue Hwa Chinese Products Emporium Ltd, 301-309 Nathan Road (at Jordan MTR station). Tel. 3-840084. As one of the larger Chinese Arts and Crafts shops is only half a block away, this makes a good store to visit and to compare prices between the two.

Small branch also near the Holiday Inn on Nathan Road.

Suggested Jewellers. See also *Factories*.

CAUSEWAY BAY

AA — *Daimaru* Department Store, Jewellery Dept, Paterson Street. Tel. 5-767321. All-around variety of goods and prices. Cat's eyes.

AA — *Diamond Creations Ltd*, Shop Q, Hong Kong Mansions, 6 Great George Street. Tel. 5-7906498.

CENTRAL

AA — *Amerex International (H.K.) Ltd*, 702 Takshing House, Des Voeux Road, C. Tel. 5-239145. Pearls. Wholesale and retail.

AA — *Anglo Tex Ltd*, 22 Des Voeux Road C., 8/F. Tel. 5-234311. Josiane Knight. Pearls and Italian gold.

AAA — *Casey Boutique*, Shop 106, Gloucester Tower, The Landmark. Tel. 5-220189. Diamonds. Designer: Raymond Chan.

AA — *Cecil Arts Jewelry Ltd*, 120 Prince's Bldg, 1/F, Ice House Street, C. Tel. 5-226811 or 5-221757.

A — *Chan Che Kee Jewellery*, 18 Pottinger Street, C. Tel. 5-226402.

AAA — *Chen Bros. Arts Co.*, Mandarin Hotel Mezz. 18, C. Tel. 5-247723.

AA — *Chow Tai Fook*, China Building G2, Queen's Road C. Tel. 5-243166. Chinese gold and jewellery.

AAA — *Dabera Ltd*, Shop 8, Swire House, Chater Road and Pedder Street. Tel. 5-236344 or 5-221280. Diamonds. Resident gemmologist and designer — Mr Baldinger, GG.

AAA — *Golay Buchel*, Room 1504, 5 Queen's Road C. Tel. 5-230151. Pearls. Jewellery designers.

A — *Honeychurch Antiques Ltd*, 29 Hollywood Road. Tel. 5-432433. Antique Chinese silver.

AA — *Jade Creations*, Lane Crawford House, 70 Queen's Road C. Tel. 5-223598. Designer, Vickie T'homi. 80% jade. Simple designs.

AA — *Kai-yin Lo*, 6 On Lan Street (off Wyndham Street, behind the Chinese Arts and Crafts). Designer originals. Tel. 5-260808.

AA — *King Fook Gold and Jewellery Co.*, 30-32 Des Voeux Road C. Tel. 5-235111. Chinese gold and jewellery.

AAA — *Lane Crawford*, 70 Queen's Road C. Tel. 5-266121. Beautiful design and craftsmanship. Antiques. Mikimoto pearls.

AA — *Manning Jewellery Co.*, 44 Queen's Road C. Tel. 5-243374 or 5-243376. Jade. South Sea pearls. Chinese gold.

AA — *Po Kwong*, 82 Queen's Road C. Tel. 5-244631 or 5-244450. Jade, South Sea pearls. Annie Osborn, FGA.

AA — *The Showroom*, Room 1203, Central Bldg, 1 Pedder Street, C. Tel. 5-257086. Diamonds, pearls, antiques and stones. Designer — Clare Wadsworth.

AA — *S.P.H. De Silva Ltd*, Shop 1, Central Bldg, Pedder Street. Tel. 5-268760. Diamonds. Coloured stones, imported enamel, cameos. Mrs Clayton, FGA, GG, appraiser.

AA — *K.S. Sze and Sons*, Mandarin Hotel. Tel. 5-242803.

A+ — *Wai Kee Jewellers*, Central Bldg, Pedder Street. Tel. 5-232285. Silver restoration.

STANLEY

A — *Ellis Jewellery Co.*, 3 Stanley New Street, by bus station. Tel. 5-930445. Small, friendly shop.

TSIM SHA TSUI

AA — *Amerex*, 5-15 Hankow Road, Rm 314. Tel. 3-686575. Pearls, Italian gold.

AAA — *Aspery of Bond St.*, Shui Hing, 23-25 Nathan Road. Tel. 3-689181 X243. Mr Penny. Antique collection.

A — *Benny Lau*, 41-43 Carnarvon Road. Tel. 3-680637.

A — *Chaumont International*, 57 Peking Road, 10/F. Tel. 3-687331. Winnie Nootenboom, FGA.

AA — *Chow Sang Sang Jewellery Co. Ltd*, 229 Nathan Road, TST. Tel. 3-683241. Chinese gold.

AA — *Chow Tai Fook*, 341 Nathan Road. Tel. 3-845164. Chinese shop. Chuk Kam gold ornaments and bullion.

AA — *Chu's Jade Manufacturer*, 1-A Kimberley Street, G/F. Tel. 3-682844.

A — *Enoch Watch Co.*, No. 34 G/F Ambassador Hotel Arcade. Tel. 3-671747. Testing, jewellery. Enoch Mau, FGA.

AAA — *Falconer Jewellers Ltd*, Main Shop, ML9-11 Mezzanine Floor, Peninsula Hotel. Tel. 3-682024 or 3-667508. Branches in

Regent and Hongkong hotels.

A — *Furama*, Ambassador Hotel Arcade. Tel. 3-678620.

AA — *Hong Kong Jade House Ltd*, 132 Ocean Terminal. Tel. 3-674516.

AA — *King Fook*, 134 Nathan Road, Miramar Hotel. Tel. 3-691281.

AAA — *Lane Crawford*, 74 Nathan Road. Tel. 3-670044.

AA — *Leung's Ivory Factory*, 37A Carnarvon Road. Tel. 3-672618. Ivory.

A — *Lo and Rador International Gem House*, Ambassador Hotel Arcade, 54 Nathan Road. Tel. 3-663003. Loose stones. Wholesale and retail.

AA — *Maggie's Jewellery Ltd*, 1/F Hyatt Regency Hotel. Tel. 3-685577. Maggie Ying — designer.

AA — *Manchu Gems*, Ocean Terminal, Shop 106, Deck 1. Tel. 3-663034.

A — *Men's Jewellery Centre*, 94 Nathan Road, G/F, Shop "K", Burlington Arcade. Tel. 3-687038 or 3-667766. Gold and silver. Women's jewellery too.

AA — *Nathan Ivory Factory*, 58 Nathan Road. Tel. 3-669687; and 81 Peking Road. Tel. 3-688914 and 3-688940. Ivory. Wholesale and retail.

A — *Papillon Jewellery Ltd*, G30-31, Tsim Sha Tsui Centre, Salisbury Road, Kowloon. Tel. 3-699348. David and Elsa Yen.

AA — *Sincere International Jewellery Co. Ltd*, No. 54 2/F Houston Centre, Mody Road. Tel. 3-689550. Peter Lee.

A — *Sunny Tsui Jewellery*, Mezz., Holiday Inn Golden Mile. Tel. 3-683674. Friendly family shop. Gem testing. Designer. Wholesale and retail.

AAA — *Trio Pearl*, Peninsula Hotel. Tel. 3-679171-4.

AA — *Vanessa*, 237/F, Ocean Terminal. Tel. 3-662288.

A — *Wing Lee Watch & Jewellery Co.*, G27B Hyatt Regency. Tel. 3-661077. Herman Chow, FGA. Gem testing.

AA — *Y.P. Lee & Sons*, 144 Ocean Terminal. Tel. 3-674563.

AA — *Yuan Feng & Co. Ltd*, 18 Ashley Road. Tel. 3-664663. Chinese antique silver.

AA — *Yuan Feng Arts & Crafts Co.*, 1A Mody Road. Tel. 3-684378. Chinese antique silver.

Foreign Brand Names

AAA — *Cartier*, Prince's Bldg, C. Tel. 5-222964; or Peninsula Hotel, TST. Tel. 3-688036.

AAA — *Chaumet*, Dickson Watch & Jewellery Co. Ltd, G/F, The Landmark, C. Tel. 5-214245-6; or G/F, The Peninsula Hotel, TST. Tel. 3-698264-6.

AAA — *Chopard Boutique*, Shop 7, G/F Central Bldg, Pedder Street, C. Tel. 5-213541-2. Swiss jewellery firm with exquisite merchandise including dress watches.

AAA — *Gianmaria Buccellati*, Lane Crawford, 70 Queen's Road C. and Peninsula Hotel, TST.

AAA — *Golay Buchel*, Rm. 1504, 5 Queen's Road C. Tel. 5-230151.

AAA — *ilias LALAoUNIS*, Susan John Ltd, R123 Lobby, Regent Hotel, TST. Tel. 3-7212811. Also Landmark.

AAA — *Mouboussin of Paris*, Casey Diamonds Boutique, Landmark, C. Tel. 5-220189.

AAA — *Nina Ricci*, Regent Hotel, R104, TST. Tel. 3-7214869.

AA — *Murat, Wilhelm Gathmann, Charles Danier*, S.P.H. De Silva Ltd, Shop 1, Central Bldg, Pedder Street, C. Tel. 5-220639. C. Tel. 5-268760.

AAA — *Van Cleef & Arpels*, G3, The Landmark, C. Tel. 5-229677; or BW-5 Peninsula Hotel, TST. Tel. 3-675544.

AAA — *Voguebijoux*, Coppola & Parodi, Lobby Floor R117, Regent Hotel, TST. Tel. 3-7211766.

WHOLESALERS/GEM DEALERS

NOTE: A wholesaler may not offer the very best price for a given item. Often a retailer with "old stock" may have it for less. One thing that the wholesaler does have is selection.

Hong Kong Gem Exchange. Tel. 5-225007. Diamonds, coloured stones. Tel. 5-246461 or 5-246462. Mr Jeremy Rex, cutter.

Lo and Rador International Gem House, Ambassador Hotel Arcade, 54 Nathan Road. Tel. 3-663003. Coloured stones, CZs, Gilson emeralds.

Mike's Company. Mike and Yvonne Wang. Tel. 3-666926 or 3-684326. Mainly African gems. Importer and cutter.

Ruppenthal (H.K.) Ltd, World Shipping Centre, 7 Canton Road, TST. Tel. 3-677304. Gems, beads. Victor Lui, Mgr. Dir.

Sapphire Gem House Ltd. Tel. 3-665763 or 3-672141 stones. M.Y. Farook.

Universal Gems. Mr Narenda Kothari, GG. Tel. 5-2 Coloured stones specialising in emeralds.

Wing Tung Trading Co. Tel. 5-443810 or 5-447534. Mr Robert C.S. Lee, GG. Direct importer of pearls from Japan. Some stones.

Siba Co., Entertainment Bldg, 14th Floor, 30 Queen's Road C. Ephraim Zion. Rare diamonds and fine jewellery. Tel. 5-2511234.

FACTORIES

Group tours may be arranged in advance, often through the HKTA. The factories listed here have agreed to visits. If you are visiting other factory showrooms, ask if you can see the work in progress. Factory showroom prices are usually very close to local retail stores. A visit to a factory is a pleasant change from crowded TST and Central.

Anju Jewelry Limited, Block B-2, 1st Floor, Kaiser Estate, 41 Man Yue Street. Hung Hom, Kowloon. Tel. 3-659081-4. Fine jewellery. Mainly wholesale, but will sell retail at factory. Mr Lucas.

John Allan Ltd, 116 Argyle Street, Capital Court, 7B, Kowloon. Tel. 3-7139271. Manufacturer, wholesaler and retailer of exclusive custom-designed jewellery. John Rae and John Yip.

Kin's Jewellery Factory, F-10, 3/F, New Port Centre, 116 Ma Tau Kok Road, Kowloon. Tel. 3-342401-4. Mr Felix Lim. Fine jewellery.

Lloyds Jewellery Co. Ltd, Freder Center, Unit B and C, L/G, 68 Sung Wong Toi Road, Kowloon. Tel. 3-341331. 14K and 18K fine jewellery, loose stones. Wholesale and retail showroom. Near airport. Julius Chang.

Tack Wing Ivory Factory, Showroom, G/F 12 Wellington Street, C. Tel. 5-242209. Wholesale and retail. Good overall prices and repair work on old pieces.

Tse Sui Luen Jewellery Co. Ltd, G/F Block B, Summit Bldg, 30 Man Yue Street. Tel. 3-334221, Miss Katherine Ho. Wholesale and retail. Manufacturers of 14K and 18K gold jewellery.

JEWELLERY SUPPLIES

For loupes and gem supplies:

Parksian Traders, 10th Floor, Chiyu Bank Bldg, 78 Des Voeux Road C. Tel. 5-246894, 5-248812.

K.T. Chow Jewellery, Hang Seng Bank Bldg, Room 1103, 19 Carnarvon Road, TST. Tel. 3-686977.

GEM CLASSES AND INSTRUCTION

Gemmological Assoc. of Hong Kong. London Preliminary Course, evenings, in English, at the Mariners Club, Middle Road, TST. Mrs Melinda Tilley, FGA. Tel. 3-638315.

Hong Kong University — General Interest Gemmology, in Cantonese.

Mrs Anne Paul, FGA, GG — General Interest Gemmology. London Preliminary and Fellowship Diploma Courses. Tel. 5-721331. Daytime classes at private residence, Mid-Levels.

Mrs Kathryn Barcham, FGA, GG — Private general interest classes. Evenings. The Peak. Tel. 5-96051.

ASSOCIATIONS

The Gemmological Association of Hong Kong. Associate membership open to the interested public. Full members must be FGA or GG. Mailing address: PO Box 97711, Tsim Sha Tsui. Tel. 5-870837. Mrs Holbrook, Secretary. Mrs Anne Paul, Chairman.

Hong Kong Gemologists Association. Limited to qualified gemmologists. PO Box 74170, Kowloon Central PO. Mr Charles Baldinger of Dabera, Chairman. Tel. 5-236344.

Hong Kong Tourist Association. For information: Tel. 3-671112. For complaints or disputes with any associate member: Tel. 5-213181.

Consumer Council. Tel. 5-747388 or 5-748297.

Consumer Advice Bureau. Tel. 5-245444.

Diamond Importers Association Ltd, Room 401, 8-10 Duddell Street, Central. Tel. 5-235497.

Hongkong Industry Dept. Tel. 3-7222333. (For Customs information if your consulate cannot help.)

Customs and Excise Dept, Hong Kong Government. Tel. 3-7222448 (for Customs information).

GEM TESTING

Gemlab, 1104 Hang Chong Bldg, No. 5 Queen's Road C. Tel. 5-225007. Appraisals, identification, diamond grading, X-rays.

Gemological Laboratory of Hong Kong, Luk Hoi Tong Bldg, Room 802, 31 Queen's Road C. Tel. 5-262422.

S.P.H. De Silva Ltd, Shop 1, Central Bldg, Pedder Street, C. Tel. 5-268760, 5-220897. Gem appraisals, gem identification, diamond grading.

Herman Chow, Wing Lee Watch and Jewellery Co., G27B Hyatt Regency Arcade, TST. Tel. 3-661077. Appraisals and identification.

H.K. Standards & Testing Centre, Eldex Indust. Bldg, 21 Ma Tau Wei Road, 12/F, Unit A, Hung Hom. Mr John Lau. Tel. 3-659061.

Dabera, Swire House, 11A Chater Road, C. Tel. 5-236344.

Asian Gem Lab, 12 Granville Road, 9/F, TST. Tel. 3-7235719.

COLOUR CHART

(of gems, imitations and synthetics found in Hong Kong)

Purple
Transparent
Almandine garnet, pyrope garnet, sapphire, star sapphire, spinel, diamond, amethyst, rhodolite garnet, topaz, tourmaline, doublets, glass, plastics, synthetic corundum, synthetic quartz
Non Transparent (opaque and translucent)
Jadeite jade, star sapphire, almandine garnet

Blue
Transparent
Topaz, tourmaline, aquamarine, sapphire, diamond, dyed quartz, synthetic corundum, synthetic quartz, doublets, triplets, foil backs
Non Transparent
Lapis lazuli, star sapphire, glass, jadeite jade, black opal, sodalite, turquoise, doublets, foil backs, glass, plastics, synthetic corundum, synthetic turquoise

Green
Transparent
Demantoid garnet, emerald, cat's eye chrysoberyl, sapphire,

tsavolite garnet, peridot, jadeite jade, chrysoprase, quartz, tourmaline, synthetic corundum, synthetic emerald, doublets, triplets, glass

Non Transparent

Beryl, dyed onyx marble, chrysoprase, cat's eye chrysoberyl, corundum, glass, jadeite jade, nephrite jade, malachite, black opal, aventurine quartz, serpentine, turquoise, synthetic emerald

Yellow

Transparent

Amber, beryl, chrysoberyl, yellow sapphire, diamond, grossularite garnet (hessonite), opal, citrine, spessartite garnet, topaz, tourmaline, doublets, triplets, foil backs, glass, plastics, synthetic corundum

Non Transparent

Amber, cat's eye chrysoberyl, jadeite jade, plastics

Orange and Brown

Transparent

Amber, beryl, chrysoberyl, corundum, diamond, grossularite garnet (hessonite), spessartite garnet, fire opal, quartz, topaz, tourmaline, triplets, glass, synthetic corundum

Non Transparent

Amber, cat's eye chrysoberyl, jadeite jade, opal, tiger's eye quartz, plastics, synthetic corundum

Pink and Red

Transparent

Almandite garnet, spinel, ruby and pink sapphire, diamond, fire opal, pyrope garnet, rose quartz, rhodolite garnet, topaz, tourmaline, doublets, triplets, foil backs, glass, plastics, synthetic corundum

Non Transparent

Star almandite garnet, coral, star ruby, grossularite, jadeite jade, synthetic corundum, foil backs, glass

White

Non Transparent

Coral, jadeite jade, nephrite jade, onyx marble, opal, glass, plastics, synthetic corundum, synthetic opal

Black
Non Transparent
Andradite garnet, black coral, black onyx, star sapphire, diamond, jadeite jade, jet, nephrite jade, opal, tourmaline, glass, doublets, plastics, synthetic opal

Grey
Non Transparent
Agate (chalcedony), star sapphire, jadeite jade, nephrite jade

Colourless
Transparent
White sapphire, diamond, rock crystal, topaz, cubic zirconium, synthetic corundum, synthetic spinel.

BIRTHSTONES

Month	Stone	Zodiac	Stone
January	Garnet	Aquarius (Jan 20-Feb 18)	Garnet
February	Amethyst	Pisces (Feb 19-Mar 20)	Amethyst
March	Aquamarine, Bloodstone	Aries (Mar 21-Apr 19)	Bloodstone
April	Diamond	Taurus (Apr 20-May 20)	Sapphire
May	Emerald	Gemini (May 21-Jun 21)	Agate
June	Pearl, Moonstone, Alexandrite	Cancer (June 22-Jul 22)	Emerald
July	Ruby, Star Ruby	Leo (Jul 23-Aug 22)	Onyx
August	Peridot, Sardonyx	Virgo (Aug 23-Sept 22)	Carnelian
September	Sapphire, Star Sapphire	Libra (Sept 23-Oct 23)	Chrysolite

October	Opal, Tourmaline	Scorpio (Oct 24-Nov 21)	Beryl
November	Topaz, Citrine	Sagittarius (Nov 22-Dec 21)	Topaz
December	Turquoise, Zircon	Capricorn (Dec 22-Jan 19)	Ruby

MOHS HARDNESS SCALE

From softest to hardest and including gems available in Hong Kong

H-1 **Talc:** soapstone (1 to 1½)

H-2 **Gypsum:** pearl and jet (2½ to 4½), serpentine (2½ to 4), amber (2 to 2½), pure gold and silver (2½ to 3)

H-3 **Calcite:** malachite, coral (3½ to 4)

H-4 **Fluorite:** synthetic opal (4½); platinum (4 to 4½)

H-5 **Apatite:** opal (5 to 6½), glass, lapis lazuli, turquoise, sodalite (5 to 6)

H-6 **Feldspar:** peridot, andradite garnet, agate and jadeite (6½ to 7), nephrite (6 to 6½)

H-7 **Quartz:** citrine, amethyst; beryl — aquamarine, emerald (7½ to 8), almandite and grossularite garnet (7½), rhodolite, spessartite and pyrope garnet, and tourmaline (7 to 7½)

H-8 **Topaz:** cat's eye chrysoberyl (8½)

H-9 **Corundum:** ruby, sapphire

H-10 **Diamond:** the hardest.

The higher number on the scale will scratch any gem below it. This test is helpful in identifying gems but it is destructive and not generally done by gemmologists. It would be more applicable to the bottoms of carvings and the backs of cabochons.

NOTE ALSO:

A fingernail will scratch anything 2 and under.

A copper coin will scratch anything 3 and under.

A pen-knife or needle will scratch anything 5 and under.

A steel industrial file will scratch anything 6 and under.

Anything 7 and higher will scratch glass.

CHINESE CALLIGRAPHY IN JEWELLERY

Especially in Hong Kong, you will encounter Chinese calligraphy in paintings, brass, porcelain, and even in some jewellery, notably gold, jade and ivory. These make a particularly special, artistic souvenir of your Hong Kong visit.

Most calligraphy refers to good luck, prosperity, longevity and happiness (usually double happiness), but you can make up a piece with your name or Chinese zodiac animal in Chinese characters.

ALL BEST WISHES COME TRUE

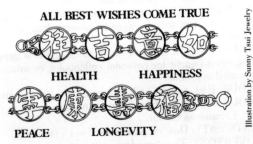

HEALTH   **HAPPINESS**

PEACE   **LONGEVITY**

Illustration by Sunny Tsui Jewelry

The Chinese believe that a succession of twelve animals governs one's life depending on the year of birth. If you are a dragon, for example, you may want to wear the character for dragon, or a dragon brooch. The animals and years are:

RAT: 1900, 1912, 1924, 1936, 1948, 1960, 1972, 1984.
OX: 1901, 1913, 1925, 1937, 1949, 1961, 1973, 1985.
TIGER: 1902, 1914, 1926, 1938, 1950, 1962, 1974.
HARE: 1903, 1915, 1927, 1939, 1951, 1963, 1975.
DRAGON: 1904, 1916, 1928, 1940, 1952, 1964, 1976.
SERPENT: 1905, 1917, 1929, 1941, 1953, 1965, 1977.
HORSE: 1906, 1918, 1930, 1942, 1954, 1966, 1978.
RAM: 1907, 1919, 1931, 1943, 1955, 1967, 1979.
MONKEY: 1908, 1920, 1932, 1944, 1956, 1968, 1980.
ROOSTER: 1909, 1921, 1933, 1945, 1957, 1969, 1981.
DOG: 1910, 1922, 1934, 1946, 1958, 1970, 1982.
BOAR or **PIG:** 1911, 1923, 1935, 1947, 1959, 1971, 1983.

GLOSSARY

BANDING: Parallel stripes of varying widths.

CABOCHON: Smoothly polished, round or oval domed gem.

C or Ct: Carat, one-twentieth of a gram. Also used in measuring gold fineness. See Karat.

CHOP: Chinese seal or stamp usually in the form of a cylinder or rectangle of glass or stone about 2″ long.

CHUK KAM: 99.99% pure gold. See *Settings, page 124.*

CLEAVAGE: The specific lines or planes along which a gem will split.

COLLECTORS': As in "collectors' stone". Finest gem quality stones, often bought for personal collections, or unusual gems rarely used in jewellery.

COLOUR: Red, orange, yellow, green, blue, purple, etc.

　BODY COLOUR: The primary colour of a pearl.

　HUE: Same as Colour.

　INTENSITY: How vivid or washed out a colour is.

　OVERTONE: The secondary colour of a gem.

　TONE: The degree of blackness. Usually described as light, medium or dark.

COSTUME JEWELLERY: Made with base metals to imitate fine jewellery or create a new fashion.

CRAZE: Crackle.

CRYSTALLINE: Clear and transparent; any gem material that has visual crystal structure bounded by flat faces.

DECORATIVE STONE: Mineral used for carvings and art objects but not normally for jewellery. Usually inexpensive and opaque.

DESIGNER: As in "designer jewellery". All jewellery is designed, but this term refers to jewellery designed by an internationally recognised jewellery company like Cartier.

EXPATRIATE: Someone residing outside his home country.

FGA: Fellow of the Gemmological Society of Great Britain.

FACET: Small, flat, cut, polished surface of a gem.

FANCIES: Generally refers to coloured diamonds.

FASHION RING: Other than fine jewellery. The setting is usually made of silver or base metals with synthetic, imitation or inexpensive stones.

FINE: As in "fine jewellery". 14K and higher settings.

FISH EYE, also WINDOW: A poorly cut gem that you can read through.

FLATS: Flat, cut and polished gem material used for jewellery or ornamental objects; without facets.

GIA: Gemological Institute of America.

GEM: See *Gems*.

GEMMOLOGIST: Someone who has passed qualifying examinations given by an internationally-recognised school for the study of gems, such as the leading Gemological Institute of America and the Gemmological Society of Great Britain.

GOLD FINENESS: Karat rating of gold in relation to alloy.

GRAIN: The line along which stones cleave; plane of atomic bonding.

HARDNESS: See Mohs hardness scale in *Appendix*.

K or Kt: Karat, one twenty-fourth of the gold content of a piece of metal. Also spelled carat (Br.). See *Gold*.

LAPIDARY: A person who cuts, polishes and works with gems, or a place where gems are cut.

LOGO: A symbol. The HKTA logo is a sailing junk.

LOUPE: A 10X magnifying glass, standard equipment of jewellers and gemmologists.

MASSIVE: Without crystal form; cryptocrystalline

MELEE: (mel-ee) Trade name for small brilliant-cut diamonds up to 20 pts used for setting around a larger stone.

NACRE: (na-cur) See *Pearl*.

ORIENT: Iridescence. Rarest quality of a pearl.

PARTI-COLOURED: More than two colours in a gem.

SCRIMSHAW: Decoration by etching or carving of bone, ivory,

etc., especially by whalers.

SYNTHETIC GEM: A man-made material with essentially the same chemical, optical and physical nature of the natural stone it duplicates.

SIMULATED or **IMITATION GEM:** Anything other than synthetic or assembled stones that imitates a natural gem. It could be glass, plastic or other non-crystal material.

TAEL: See *Gold.*

ULTRASONIC CLEANER: See *Care and Protection of Jewellery, page 129.*

ZONING: Patches of colour within a gem; usually considered undesirable.

BIBLIOGRAPHY

Arem, Joel E.: *Gems and Jewelry*. Ridge Press, NYC. 1975.

Arem, Joel E.: *Color Encyclopedia of Gemstones*. Van Nostrand Reinhold, NYC. 1977.

Chu, Arthur and Grace: *The Collectors Book of Jade*. Crown Publishing, NYC. 1978.

Cudlipp, Edythe: *Jewelry, an Appreciation of Luxury, Guide to Value*. E.P. Dutton, NYC. 1980.

Liddicoat, Richard T. Jr. and Copeland, Lawrence L.: *The Jewelers' Manual*. Gemological Institute of America, Los Angeles. 1974.

Richardson, Wally and Huett, Lenora: *Spiritual Value of Gem Stones*. DeVorss & Co., Marina del Rey, Cal. 1980.

Schumann, Walter: *Gemstones of the World*. Sterling Pub. Co. Inc., NYC. 1977-1979.

Webster, Robert: *Gems, their Sources, Descriptions and Identification*. Butterworths, London and Boston. 1980.